ROAMING THE BACK ROADS

Dedicated by Carol Holleuffer
    to my father, whose shortcuts became family legend,
    and to my mother, who couldn't read maps but
    welcomed the unexpected.
    These are the roads they knew.

Dedicated by Peter Browning
    to the guy who invented second gear
    and the illegal U-turn.

ROAMING THE BACK ROADS

DAY TRIPS BY CAR
THROUGH NORTHERN CALIFORNIA

TEXT BY PETER BROWNING

ILLUSTRATED WITH MAPS AND
PHOTOGRAPHS BY CAROL HOLLEUFFER

CHRONICLE BOOKS
SAN FRANCISCO

Cover Photo by Peter Browning.
Composition by Hansen & Associates.

Library of Congress Cataloging in Publication Data

Browning, Peter, 1928-
  Roaming the back roads.

  1. California—Description and travel—1951-
—Tours.   2. San Francisco Bay region—Description
and travel—Tours.   3. Automobiles—Road guides—
California.   4. Automobiles—Road guides—California
—San Francisco Bay region.   I. Holleuffer, Carol.
II. Title.
F859.3.B68   917.94′04′5   78-27569
ISBN 0-87701-128-1

Chronicle Books
870 Market Street
San Francisco, CA 94102

CONTENTS

Marin to the Sonoma Coast

Wine Country to the Geysers

Carquinez, the Delta, and Contra Costa

Santa Cruz Mountains, the Coast, and Old San Juan

Take the Long Way Around

We have often thought, while observing the desperate driving maneuvers so many people employ to gain a few seconds' advantage over other drivers, that the most crucial lesson of driving behavior has been forgotten—or, perhaps, never learned. That lesson is: You are almost never in a desperate hurry. And, if you are not, then why do you hurry? And why, instead of rushing in order to shorten your trip, shouldn't you deliberately lengthen it? And if you can do that, then go one step further and make the trip itself —rather than the end of the trip—your goal.

These back-road tours vary considerably in length. Some, if you did nothing but drive, would be over in an hour. Others require half a day or a full day. Much depends on how devoted you are to taking your time about it. If you cannot squelch the urge to "make time," you may gain minutes or hours to devote to some other restless activity but you will have gained nothing of what your tour has to offer.

Some of the tours go to or pass by historic sites or other places of interest. Others are mainly *drives* that do not take you to a particular place, but rather are to be enjoyed for the scenery and for the quiet pleasure of having eluded the madding crowd. Some trips will occupy a day in themselves, but can also be done in conjunction with other things. For instance, if you are visiting the wineries of Napa County, you can enhance your wine-tasting by taking the Pope Valley-Aetna Springs trip, or the Silverado Mine-Great Western Mine Road loop out of Calistoga.

Have you ever wondered how to entertain visiting relatives once they have seen all the standard tourist sights? Have you ever racked your brain trying to think of a pleasant activity for someone who cannot do strenuous things? Have you grown bored with driving the same roads over and over again, and wished there were some new route to arouse your interest and curiosity? If so, then your troubles are over, for you're holding the answer to those questions in your hand.

The maps in this book have been made to supplement a California state road map. No other maps are necessary, though if you have something more detailed you may be able to create variations on the routes we have described. If you are an AAA member, get their maps; they are the best.

All of these trips were made between January and June of 1978. The information in this book was accurate as of that time. Keep in mind that road conditions, hours, and rates and fees do change. We hope that you will be in a relaxed frame of mind while touring. There are many quiet back roads and many sights to see.

Most of the historical and place-name information in the descriptions of these trips comes from three books. We highly recommend them to anyone interested in California history—or in pleasant and informative reading. They are:

Farquhar, Francis P. (ed.). *Up and Down California in 1860-1864, The Journal of William H. Brewer.* Berkeley and Los Angeles, University of California Press, 1966.
William Brewer was a member of the original California Geological Survey, under the leadership of Josiah Dwight Whitney. The book is available in most libraries, and can also be found in paperback in many bookstores.

Hoover, Mildred B., Rensch, Eugene H., and Rensch, Ethel G. *Historic Spots in California.* Third Edition, revised by William N. Abeloe. Stanford, Stanford University Press, 1966.
The only complete guide to the historical landmarks of California. There is an incredible wealth of information in these 600 pages, making you wonder how the authors managed to put it all together. The book is still in print, and is available in most libraries.

Gudde, Erwin G. *California Place Names.* Second Edition. Berkeley and Los Angeles, University of California Press, 1960.
This book is available in most libraries as a reference work.

Also of great value is a pamphlet, *California Historical Landmarks,* available for two dollars at state historical sites and monuments, or from the Department of Parks and Recreation, P.O. Box 2390, Sacramento, CA 95811.

We wish you safe and pleasant traveling.

Carol Holleuffer
Peter Browning

8   ROAMING THE BACK ROADS

Petaluma-
Point Reyes Station

Three miles northeast of the town of Petaluma, on a knoll with a sweeping view of the Petaluma Valley, is the largest adobe structure in northern California. It is the Petaluma Adobe, built between 1836 and 1846, once the central building for Rancho Petaluma, the 66,000-acre estate of General Mariano Guadalupe Vallejo.

The adobe is now a state historic park. A great deal of excellent restoration has been done, but nevertheless 85 percent of the walls and 20 percent of the woodwork are original. There are interpretive exhibits at the visitor center, and many rooms are furnished with authentic pieces from the California rancho era. Rancho Petaluma once covered the area between Sonoma Creek and Petaluma Creek, and from San Pablo Bay north to Glen Ellen and almost to Cotati. Cattle-raising was the most important activity, but there were also sheep and horses, and crops of grain were grown for local use and for trade. The adobe contained living quarters and storerooms, a weaving shop, and a blacksmith shop.

To get to the Petaluma Adobe take U.S. 101 to State Route 116 East near Petaluma. There are state historic signs on 101 before the exit, and signs on route 116 that lead you to the adobe—three miles from the exit. (Hours are 10 to 5; admission is fifty cents per person, free for those under 18; the tours are self-guiding; and there is an attractive picnic area beside a stream bed at the foot of the knoll. The phone number is (707) 762-4871.)

When you leave the adobe, return the way you came but do not get onto 101. Instead, go under 101 and continue into Petaluma on Lakeville Street. Though the name Petaluma has a Spanish ring to it, it is of Indian derivation, meaning either "flat back" (referring to a low hill east of the creek where there was once an Indian village), or simply "flat place." There was a Mexican colony at Petaluma in 1833, and a Yankee settlement that dates from the early 1850s. Petaluma's rise to prominence began in 1878 when Lyman Rice, a young Canadian, decided that the region was suited to chicken-raising. He sent away to Canada for some white leghorns, and began the industry that made Petaluma "The World's Egg Basket"—or "Chickaluma," as the rustic wits used to say. But that's in the past. Though there are still some egg ranches in the vicinity of Petaluma, egg production is no longer the dominant industry. However, Petaluma has a flair for the unusual. It's the site of the National Arm-Wrestling competition, and of the Ugly Dog Contest. So teach your ugly dog to arm wrestle, and put him on the next bus to Petaluma.

About a mile after passing under the freeway turn left on D Street and go straight through town and on south. The street name soon changes to Red Hill Road, and when you cross into Marin County it changes again to Petaluma–Point Reyes Road. Under any name it is a pleasant drive through rolling green hills. Nine miles from Petaluma is the Marin French Cheese Company. A very interesting and informative free guided tour begins every half hour from 10 to 4. In the salesroom you may purchase short-weighted packages of cheese at reduced prices (but not reduced in quality), and also bread, wine, and other edibles. There is a large picnic area. (Hours are 9 to 5 daily; closed on some holidays.)

If you wish to make a short loop and return to Petaluma and Highway 101, go back the way you came and—in about a mile—turn left on Wilson Hill Road. Go right at the junction with the Marshall-Petaluma Road, and it's eight miles back to Petaluma.

If you have the time there is a longer and more interesting way to return to Petaluma. Continue on south from the cheese company. The road winds up and over a ridge and past the Nicasio Reservoir. Turn right at the three-way stop below the reservoir, and in three miles you come to State Route 1. Turn left and go to the town of Point Reyes Station. Continue two miles on south of town on route 1, and turn right on Bear Valley Road. About a half a mile down the road is the headquarters of the Point Reyes National Seashore. Many guidebooks provide information on Point Reyes, but at the headquarters you can get all the information you want for free—roads, trails, beaches, what to do and see. For something out of the ordinary we recommend the self-guided earthquake trail along the San Andreas Fault

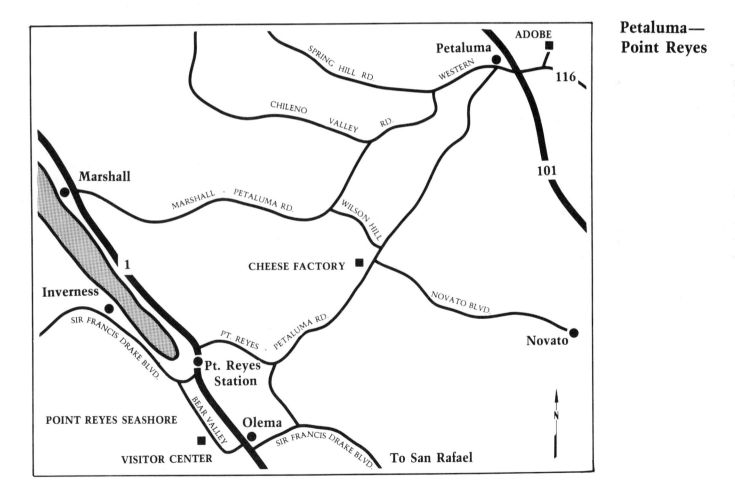

The courtyard of Petaluma Adobe. Hides and tallow were the major products of General Vallejo's rancho.

near the headquarters, and a visit to the Johnson Oyster Company's farm on Drake's Estero. For further information, write to the Superintendent, Point Reyes National Seashore, Point Reyes, CA 94956.

To continue the trip go north from Point Reyes Station on route 1, which runs along Tomales Bay. You pass several tiny communities—Bivalve, Millerton, Marconi, Reynolds—and if you keep a close watch you will be able to see, at various places, the right of way of the old North Pacific Coast Railroad. The tracks usually were at the water's edge, often on embankments or trestles. Part of a trestle can be seen just beyond the buildings at Marshall, and the line of the railroad curves out around a point.

Just past Marshall turn right on the Marshall–Petaluma Road. From here it's twenty miles to Petaluma, a fine road for a slow drive through some of the loveliest and most isolated part of Marin County. As you climb up toward Bolinas Ridge there are good views back to Tomales Bay. You wind over hills and down into valleys on a little-used road through sheep- and cattle-grazing country. At the Chileno Valley Road (*Chileno*: a native of Chile) you take the right fork—which is actually straight ahead toward Petaluma, and as you near town the road comes to a deadend at Western Avenue. Turn right and follow Western into town, turn left at Petaluma Boulevard (a traffic signal), go one block, and turn right on Washington Street, which takes you out to U.S. 101.

If you have a copy of Sonoma County Farm Trails, you're all set—or you can get one at the Chamber of Commerce, which you pass at 314 Western Avenue. Here are a few places that you might want to visit:

Buchan Oyster Company
520 Cleveland Lane (763-4161)
Packing plant and retail store. Open all year. Monday-Friday, 8 to 5; weekends, 10 to 5.

Petaluma Mushroom Farm
782 Thompson Lane (762-1280)
Fresh mushrooms. Spent compost. Open all year. Tuesday-Saturday, 9 to 5; Sunday, 12 to 5.

Miller Ranches Egg Store
700 Cavanaugh Lane (763-0921)
Fresh eggs. Open all year. Monday-Friday, 9 to 5; Saturday, 9 to 3.

Central Sonoma County Loop

In an easy half day you can sample several kinds of terrain, pass through a region that has experienced two or three kinds of economic life in little more than a century, and follow the route of a vanished railroad.

All of this is to be found on a loop west of U.S. 101 between Cotati and Healdsburg. Going northbound on 101 from San Francisco, take the Railroad Avenue exit about five miles north of Petaluma. Go under the freeway to Stony Point Road, turn right, and in one and a half miles you will come to the Washoe House, an unpretentious building on the left side of the road. This is the oldest operating roadhouse in California. It was built in 1859 as a hotel and stage stop, halfway between Petaluma and Santa Rosa. It is now a bar and restaurant, and even if you have no need to take on provisions or wet your whistle, step inside and look around. Lunch is served from 11 to 2, dinner from 6 to 10, and prices are moderate.

From the Washoe House go west on Roblar Road about eight miles to the junction with the Petaluma–Valley Ford Road. Turn right and drive for seven tenths of a mile and then turn right again on Bloomfield Road. Bloomfield is a choice spot for photographers. Along one side of the road are a tavern, Masonic Hall, and other buildings, which once comprised the business district. On the other side of the road is a field where cattle graze. It's an old town, first settled in 1855 and originally called Blumefield, after a Dr. Blume, an early German pioneer in Sonoma County. Somewhere along the line the name was anglicized to Bloomfield. About two miles north of town turn left on Burnside Road, which climbs to a hilltop crowned with a grove of eucalyptus. There are good views in all directions. You descend to meet Barnett Valley Road at a stop sign. Go left two miles to Bodega Highway, and left again to Freestone. Turn right on Bohemian Highway and go into the village.

Freestone acquired its name from a nearby sandstone quarry. It's on the route of the North Pacific Coast Railroad, which operated between Sausalito and Cazadero from the 1870s to 1930. You can still see two of the old railroad cars in the village. Across the road from these is the Freestone House, a former hotel that is now an antique store (closed Mondays). Next to the hotel, and in the grounds around it, is the Wishing Well Nursery, featuring a latticework gazebo (closed Tuesdays). When this section of the railroad was being built, the local innkeeper did a fine business by boarding the construction crews. As the line moved north, the crews moved with it. The ambitious innkeeper saw his prosperity waning. He came up with an aggressive but foolish scheme for retaining his clientele. At night he went out and burned the bridges that the crews had erected during the day. He was caught and sent to San Quentin for a stretch as penalty for excessive free enterprise.

From Freestone north to the Russian River you will follow the general route of the railroad. The Bohemian Highway to Occidental and Monte Rio takes its name from the Bohemian Club of San Francisco, which held its first summer encampment in a grove of redwoods near the Russian River in 1878. The railroad had to cross several ravines in the four miles from Freestone to Howard's (now Occidental). One of these timber bridges, across Brown's Canyon, was 137 feet above the stream bed, and was at that time the highest bridge west of the Mississippi.

Occidental, once a lumber and railroad town, is now best known for its three family-style Italian restaurants. Continue on north out of town on Bohemian Highway, which follows along Dutch Bill Creek through second-growth redwoods—country that was cut over between 1870 and 1910. In seven miles you come to Monte Rio, on the Russian River. You may look at that name and think "Mountain River"—but that would be Italian, not Spanish. A free translation from Spanish would give "River Grove," or "Trees-Along-the-River."

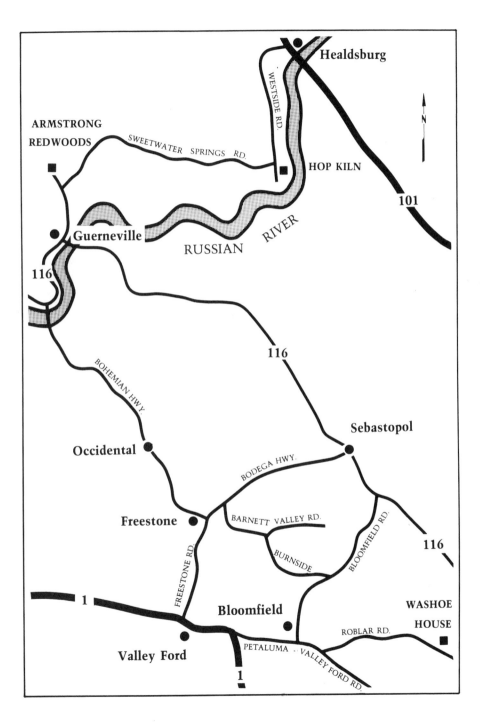

Central Sonoma Loop

17

Cross the river and turn right on State Route 116. This is, unfortunately, a heavily traveled road, especially on summer weekends. But you'll be on it only four miles to Guerneville, so grit your teeth and think pleasant thoughts of isolated country roads.

Guerneville (pronounced *Gurnville* so the locals won't know you're a stranger) also was a lumber town and—for a short time—a mining center of sorts with two nearby quicksilver mines employing five hundred people. The town was named for George Emile Guerne, an Ohioan who built a sawmill here in 1864. It has a growing permanent population, but it's main business is tourism. In summer and on weekends the population seems to increase by a factor of ten.

We'd like to get you away from concrete and traffic jams, so turn left at the stop sign where route 116 goes right. There is also a sign pointing left to Armstrong Redwoods State Reserve. The reserve is just two miles from Guerneville, and the transition from resort town to virgin redwood forest may come as a shock. (Baron Alexander von Humboldt, the great German explorer, once wrote that it was not possible to pass from Siberia into Senegal without losing consciousness. The same might be said for passing from Guerneville to the redwood forest.)

Colonel James Armstrong, a lumberman, had the good sense to set aside this 680 acres of virgin forest. You may find it hard to believe, but before lumbermen came this way there were forests like this on all the bottom land of the Russian River and along the creeks flowing into it. For the contemporary traveler there is a large picnic area and a self-guided nature trail. (Day use fee is $1.50.)

From the Armstrong Redwoods entrance station go back south a fourth of a mile and turn left on Sweetwater Springs Road. If you had been thinking of cutting the tour short at this point, don't do it. The next eight to ten miles are over the most isolated stretch of road on this entire route. The road is flat for a mile, then climbs up past a photogenic old mine—not operating, but with many buildings intact—switches back up over a low ridge, and after a dip climbs over a higher ridge. On a clear day you'll have a great vista across a valley to Mount St. Helena and the Mayacmas Mountains, a good twenty miles away.

There are many spots to picnic as you descend into the valley. For about three miles you follow Porter Creek, passing through an old farm, weatherbeaten but still operating. The creek dips south, and the road climbs once again over grassy hills before going down to the junction with Westside Road. A left turn takes you back to Healdsburg, but first make a slight detour to the Hop Kiln Winery. You can see it from the junction. Turn right and continue for a quarter of a mile. The winery is the huge barn-like building with three chimneys on top.

Back in the good old days, when beer was made with hops and other *real* ingredients rather than the ersatz materials now used, there were many hop kilns in Sonoma County. Only a few remain. This kiln has been put to another worthy purpose: the making of 100 percent varietal wines. Tours, tasting, and picnics. (Open Saturdays and Sundays, 10 to 5.)

Reverse your course on Westside Road and head for Healdsburg, ten miles away, and a connection with U.S. 101. Healdsburg is a good place to start on several other trips: Dry Creek-Stewarts Point; The Geysers; Pine Flat and Chalk Hill Roads. Fill up on gas, food, and refreshing beverages, and get started. If you do all the trips in this book in succession, you'll get into the Guinness Book of Records—or into a home for the feeble-minded.

Tomales
to Bridge Haven

From Tomales to Bridge Haven via State Route 1 is twenty-four miles. For a few extra miles and twice as much time you can go between those two points on country roads without ever feeling obliged to drive over thirty-five miles per hour.

The origin of the name Tomales is in doubt. One theory says it's a Spanish corruption of a Coast Miwok word meaning "bay." Another idea suggests it's an Indian adaptation of the Spanish word "tamal." A third theory has "tamal" as the Miwok word for "west"—meaning the people who lived along the coast to the west. Take your pick—it's a free country.

The early economic development of northern Marin and southern Sonoma counties was greatly enhanced by the construction of railroads in the nineteenth century. The North Pacific Coast Railroad, a narrow gauge line, was built in the 1870s. It ran from Sausalito to Point Reyes Station, Tomales, Valley Ford, the Russian River, and ended at Cazadero. The line was abandoned in 1930, but traces of it still remain—as you will see on this tour and on the Marshall–Point Reyes Station loop.

Dairy farming is the predominant activity hereabouts, but the early settlers raised oats, wheat, and—especially—potatoes. There was one particular variety known as "Bodega Reds," for their bright maroon coats beneath rough skins. These potatoes were in great demand by San Franciscans, who in the 1800s received shipments by boat from a port on Tomales Bay. In those days, potatoes meant Irishmen. William H. Brewer, a member of the original California Geological Survey, made a walking trip from Petaluma to Tomales in November of 1862, and had the misfortune to spend a night in Tomales. He wrote:

> The place was filled with the Irish potato diggers, all as lively as the poorest whiskey could make them. One Irishman had just made some two hundred dollars by a contract for digging, and was celebrating the event, freely treating—in fact, he was just at the culmination of a three days' spree. The 'rooms' of the house were far from private, the beds not highly inviting, and the customers twice as many as the accommodations. Drunkenness, singing, fighting, and the usual noise of Irish sprees were kept up through the night. Much to my disgust I had neither 'bowie' nor 'Colt' along, so could not command the exemption from meddling which those companions would have insured. Now, I don't mind the discomforts of the *field*, of sleeping on the ground, of diet, dust, lizards, snakes, ants, tarantulas, etc., but from drunken Irishmen, from Irish groggeries, from 'ladies' of that description, 'Good Lord, deliver us!'

As you are headed north on route 1, turn left on Dillon Beach Road at Tomales. In about a mile turn right on Middle Road, and it's six miles to Valley Ford across treeless hills. In a couple of miles you'll come to the junction with Whitacker Bluff Road. It's not a standard four-way intersection, but rather a curve to the right, back to the left, then a right turn. You will still be on Middle Road and still headed north. About half a mile before Valley Ford a section of the old railroad trestle stands in a low field on your left. At one time the trestle went entirely across this low ground and the Estero Americano—the creek that is the Marin–Sonoma county line.

At the junction with State Route 1 turn left into Valley Ford, a small town based on the dairy industry. An old Indian and Spanish trail crossed the Estero here, which gave the town its name. Food and gas are available, and the local Bank of America is an odd building—looking nothing at all like a branch of the world's largest commercial bank.

Keep on going through town for a third of a mile and turn right on the Valley Ford–Freestone Road. It follows the route of the old narrow gauge, and if you look hard you may detect—or think you detect—portions of the right of way. After two and a half miles turn left on Bodega Road. The

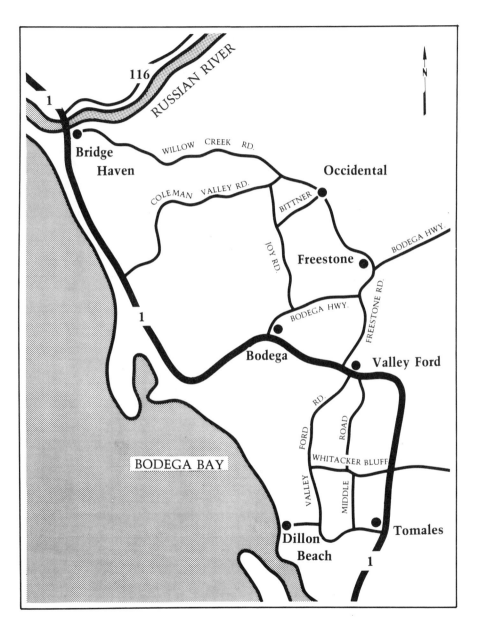

Watson School Wayside Park is about a mile or so down the road, on the left-hand side. It's a good spot for a picnic lunch. The old school, built in 1856, is preserved, and there are restrooms and a few tables. The school is perhaps the only memorial to James Watson, who did so well selling Bodega Reds that he acquired thousands of acres of land—and even had a private horse-racing track.

Another mile brings you to Joy Road, where you turn right. But first you may want to continue on for another mile to Bodega to see St. Teresa's Catholic Church, built in the early 1860s, and the Potter School, built in 1873. The school was featured in the Hitchcock movie *The Birds*.

Return to Joy Road, which heads due north and soon climbs into the redwood forest belt. All of this redwood country was much more heavily timbered before the arrival of American settlers. The extensive lumbering from 1870 to about 1910 consumed most of the commercial timber, and the lumber companies moved farther north. Joy Road runs atop a ridge for about three miles, then you turn right on Bittner Road which goes downhill into Occidental—the only town in the United States to bear this name. The town took its name from a Methodist Church built here in 1876, but until 1891 the railroad station was called Howard's, after an early settler. To the trainmen of the North Pacific Coast Railroad, the place was simply The Summit—at 570 feet above sea level the highest point on the line. Occidental started as a logging town, but is now noted chiefly for its three family-style Italian restaurants: the Union Hotel (built in 1876), Negri's, and Fiori's. Good food and lots of it are what they serve. On weekends they are crowded, and so is the town.

When you leave Occidental head west on Coleman Valley Road. This is one way to go to the coast. A couple of miles out of town it becomes narrow and runs along a ridge through sheep-grazing country, before descending to meet route 1. On a weekday it's a pleasant drive, but on weekends it is used as a through route to the beaches and can be crowded. It's not a route we recommend anyway, except in wet weather.

About a mile and a half out of Occidental turn right on Willow Creek Road. (This is the dry-weather route; if it's raining, follow Coleman Valley Road.) The first two miles are paved and run past scattered houses, and then there are five miles of good dirt and gravel. The road zigzags along the hillside above Willow Creek at first, then descends to follow the creek when the valley widens out. Around the turn of the century the North Pacific Coast built a logging spur up Willow Creek. You pass through a mixed forest of bay and redwood trees, with blue ceanothus and wild iris, but there are many enormous redwood stumps to give you a hint of the dark and dense forest it must have been before it was logged over.

As the valley widens you pass through a couple of farms and come to pavement again. After crossing the creek three times you meet route 1 at Bridge Haven, just at the south end of the bridge across the Russian River. Cross the bridge to the junction with State Route 116. From there, Jenner is one mile to the left and Guerneville thirteen miles to the right. If you are making this trip in reverse, Willow Creek Road turns off route 1 at the Bridge Haven restaurant and Union 76 station.

Railroad buffs and those interested in learning about the early history of this region should head for the nearest library and get a copy of *Narrow Gauge to the Redwoods*, by A. Bray Dickinson. It's the definitive work on the North Pacific Coast Railroad, and is well written and wonderfully illustrated.

Dry Creek-
Stewarts Point

The Skaggs Springs–Stewarts Point Road, which in forty miles takes you from U.S. 101 west to State Route 1 on the coast, is a road you should take sooner rather than later. There is a possibility that part of it will be inundated by the waters that will form behind Warm Springs Dam. Though a new road will be built higher up, a good eight miles of the present road will be lost.

The first part of this trip can be used simply as an alternate route to U.S. 101—a chance to get off the freeway for half an hour. Going north on 101, take the Healdsburg exit. Harmon G. Heald established a trading post here in 1846. For a few years in the 1850s the town was called Russian River (named after you know who, from the river of the same name which the Spanish had called San Ygnacio.) Many of the earlier inhabitants of Healdsburg were Italian grape-growers.

Go to the first traffic light—Mill Street—and turn left. Cross the railroad tracks, go under the freeway, cross the creek, and turn right at the next opportunity, on West Dry Creek Road. This is a slow-driving route, one that never goes straight if it can make a bend. Unlike the places that most of us are used to, there isn't anything that looks as if it was just built yesterday, or even much that has been built since the Second World War. You pass orchards and vineyards and old farms, and except for meeting an occasional vehicle you could be back in the last century. Across the valley is Dry Creek Road, which runs parallel to West Dry Creek Road. It's a more modern track and only for those who think they're engaged in some urgent business.

In about ten miles you turn right on Yoakim Bridge Road and cross the creek to Dry Creek Road at the stop sign. Turn left (a sign reads Stewarts Point 38), and in about a mile and a half turn right on Dutcher Creek Road. This will take you to U.S. 101 about three miles south of Cloverdale. You go straight from here to get to the coast over a good but little-used route, the Skaggs Springs–Stewarts Point Road.

In a mile you jog left across Warm Creek, and shortly you'll see a long bridge high overhead—a roadway as yet unused, awaiting construction of the dam that will flood Warm Springs Valley. Work on the dam has been stopped since 1974 by an environmental suit, and it is uncertain whether it will ever be completed.

About two miles farther on you pass the site of Skaggs Springs, once a famous hot springs resort. Two brothers built the resort in 1864, and it prospered to become next in importance and popularity to The Geysers. Guests took the Northwest Pacific Railroad to Geyserville, where they were met by carriages that conveyed them the nine miles to Skaggs Springs. There were accommodations for at least three hundred people, who paid $2 a day or $10 to $12 a week, a price that included room, board, and use of all the baths. A guidebook of 1881 mentioned the ". . . hot sulphur springs and a springs for bathing, while there is also a cold soda and iron spring, which proves an excellent tonic for invalids; the principal attractions are its positively luxurious baths." It is all gone now, which seems a great shame. But the indolent pleasures of the old spas—taking the waters, croquet, lawn tennis—couldn't compete with the great array of amusements and diversions available to the present generations.

The road follows the creek in a shallow canyon, and after several miles climbs over a ridge where sheep are grazing and you have a view of the surrounding countryside. The land is relatively undisturbed: a bit of stock-grazing, and little else. Often the road is just a lane and a half wide, and there are more turns than you can count on all your fingers and toes, but there isn't much competition from other cars. The road runs alongside Wolf Creek, a tributary of the Gualala River, for a number of miles.

After you've gone about thirty of the thirty-eight miles on this road, turn right on Annapolis Road, which crosses the creek on an old steel bridge. You can't miss it. It's the first bridge and the first possible place to turn off. To get to the coast in the shortest time, go straight ahead to Stewarts Point

Dry Creek— Stewarts Point

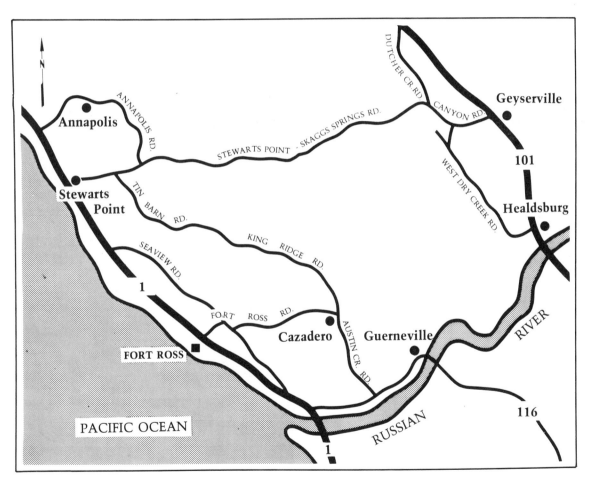

*Stewarts Point,
one of the doghole ports
that flourished at the end
of the nineteenth century*

—but why not take the long way around? You climb steeply away from the creek and loop up and down over the hills to Annapolis.

Like many other communities in this part of the state, Annapolis was once an active lumber town. That industry met the common fate: the best commercial timber was cut; the lumbermen moved north; and in 1918 the local sawmill was destroyed by fire. Annapolis isn't big enough to be called a village, but there must be a greater population in the vicinity than is apparent to the passerby. There is a post office—and for a place to have a zip code means that it's a *real* place, even if the post office is a weather-beaten, one-room shack. It has just the sort of quaint charm to make you whip out your camera—except that someone with no soul has plunked a modern telephone booth down on the front porch.

Beyond Annapolis you descend to the confluence of the two major forks of the Gualala River. The South Fork of the Gualala is peculiar in that it parallels the coast for about fifteen miles. It runs directly along the San Andreas Fault—the shattered rock of the fault zone eroded more quickly than the surrounding rock and became a natural watercourse. In a couple of miles you come to State Route 1 and the coast. To the left four miles is Stewarts Point: a few frame houses, a general store built in 1868, and an old schoolhouse. This was once a lumber center and what was called a "doghole port." From the rocky point at the edge of the cove, railroad ties and planks slid down a wooden chute to schooners below—a tricky business in dangerous waters that resulted in several shipwrecks around the turn of the century.

There were three loading chutes in the 1870s, but later only one—which was used into the early 1900s. Stewarts Point and the other doghole ports on this coast flourished from about 1874 to 1900. After the turn of the century, shipments of timber products were made increasingly by other means—first by rail, and then by logging truck. The ports were out of business entirely by the end of the twenties.

Stewarts Point is the end of this tour. If you're game for some more back-roads driving, and want to make a grand circle tour to return to U.S. 101, then the Tin Barn Road–King Ridge route is just what you're after. So stock up on food and drink at the Stewarts Point store and head out for some of the loveliest rural country in California.

Cazadero-
Fort Ross-
Stewarts Point

The road to Cazadero leaves State Route 116 about seven miles downriver from Guerneville. Actually there are two roads. The more modern one turns off just west of the bridge across Austin Creek. That is, if you're coming from Guerneville, cross the bridge and then turn right on Cazadero Highway. This follows roughly the line of the old North Pacific Coast Railroad. A mile before Cazadero you pass through Elim Grove, (*Elim* is *mile*, backwards) the favorite picnic spot of the weekend excursionists from San Francisco in the late nineteenth and early twentieth centuries.

The other route, Austin Creek Road, turns off 116 just before the bridge. For three miles there are many summer homes along the creek in an area of second growth redwoods. This has been a resort area since the late 1800s when it was logged. Though the present redwoods are nothing like the size of their predecessors, they provide enough shade to make this a dark and cool spot even on a hot summer day. At three miles you cross a bridge to a stop sign at Cazadero Highway. Turn right, and you'll be in town in no time.

Cazadero was originally a logging center, and in the 1880s became the terminus of the North Pacific Coast Railroad. The name is American Spanish meaning 'hunting place.' With all the windings of the road, and the surrounding hills and forests, you may feel that you have gained considerable altitude—but Cazadero is only 117 feet above sea level.

Go straight through town, and at the junction bear left on the Fort Ross Road; it's thirteen miles to Fort Ross from here. As you climb away from town and pass over a ridge you leave the redwoods and get into a brushy, logged-over area. Ten miles from Cazadero is Meyers Grade Road, which goes back south for five miles and connects with route 1. This is another way to begin this trip if you are coming up the coast on route 1 and don't want to go by way of Cazadero. Meyers Grade Road turns right off route 1 six miles north of Jenner. It climbs steeply through sheep-grazing country to the ridge. On the way up, look back and to your left for great views of the Sonoma coast.

From the Fort Ross Road–Meyers Grade Road junction continue north another half mile on Fort Ross Road, which then turns left and goes downhill. (The road straight ahead from this point is called Seaview Road.) The Fort Ross Road is steep and narrow and has little traffic—much of it is one lane though it is a two-way road. You cross the San Andreas Fault shortly before the base of the hills. In this area the 1906 earthquake plowed a number of parallel furrows in the ground, and displaced fences by up to fifteen feet. Hold on to your hats.

The parking area for the Fort Ross State Historical Park is directly ahead of you across route 1. It's open 9 to 6 in summer, 9 to 5 in winter. Admission is fifty cents—money well spent. The old coast highway ran through the fort site. You park well away from the fort and have a five- to ten-minute walk on the old road to reach it. It's an easy, enjoyable stroll, suitable for people of all ages, and if it's the appropriate hour carry a picnic lunch down with you.

The Russians arrived here in 1812 and erected an outpost of their Alaska settlements. The name Ross (Rossiya), an archaic, poetical way of saying "Russians," was chosen at random by the settlers from lots placed at the base of an image of Christ. Much of the Russians' activity was directed toward supplying food and other goods for Alaska. In 1814 they established the first tannery in California, and from the tanned hides made soles and uppers for boots. A small portion of these were traded to the Spanish, but most were shipped to the Russian base at Sitka. Early in 1842 the Russians sold the fort and herds of sheep and cattle to John Sutter of Sutter's Fort, and then pulled out. For some sixty years the buildings at Fort Ross were used for various purposes by several owners. In 1903 the fort was acquired by the California Historical Landmarks Committee; it was turned over to the state three years later.

From about 1875 to the early 1900s Fort Ross Landing was one of the doghole ports of this part of the coast. There was a wharf at the foot of the bluff on the north side of the cove, and a chute 180 feet long for loading the ships. It was an active place in its time. The figures for 1877 show that eighty-six vessels were loaded here. Together they carried 32,783 posts, 1548 cords of firewood, and 1619 cords of tanbark.

There are two ways to go from here to Stewarts Point. Go north on route 1 about two and one half miles to Timber Cove Road, where you turn right and climb steeply to join Seaview Road on the ridge. Timber Cove also was a doghole port. A lumber mill was established here in 1859, and as early as November 1861 a schooner took a load of tanbark to Sacramento. The loading chute was on the northwest side of the cove.

Turn left on Seaview Road, and in three miles you come to Plantation—an unlikely place name for California. It was named after a roadhouse erected here in the nineteenth century. The ranch buildings, which are now a private summer camp, are right in the center of the earthquake fault zone. (If you aren't yet nervous about earthquakes, it's too late to start now.)

Shortly past Plantation go left on Kruse Ranch Road. It's four miles down to route 1. Part of this is dirt, which in the spring is often rough and rutted, but still quite passable in any passenger car. You don't want to miss this road, as it takes you through the Kruse Rhododendron State Reserve. This is maintained in its natural state, with rhododendrons growing twenty to thirty feet high. They bloom from mid-May to mid-June. There are hiking trails and a nature trail to encourage you to get out of your car and stroll about.

Just north of the junction of Kruse Ranch Road and route 1 is Fisk Mill Cove, one of the lesser doghole ports. The chute was at the tip of the southerly point at the cove's western end. Another five miles up the coast on route 1 is Stewarts Point.

The other route from Timber Cove is the obvious one—straight up the coastal highway. A mile and a half above Timber Cove is Stillwater Cove County Park. (Picnicking, beachcombing, day use $1.50.) The Fort Ross school, removed from its original location, is here and is fully restored. It's about a ten-minute walk from the parking area. The signs were not yet up in the spring of 1978, and you may have to ask a ranger for directions.

Another three miles up the coast is Salt Point State Park. (Picnicking, hiking trails, day use $1.50.) In the late nineteenth century Salt Point had a modest lumber business. A mill was erected in 1872 in Miller Gulch (on Miller Creek) just north of Salt Point. From the mill a wooden-railed tramway was built to the point, running between the present road and the ocean. Lumber was hauled along the tramway on horse-drawn flatcars to the Salt Point loading chute, which came off the top of a 35-foot cliff. There also was rock quarrying in the 1880s and 1890s; some of the rocks were used for curbstones along the streets of San Francisco.

Two miles farther north is the Stump Beach picnic area, and two more miles north of that is Kruse Ranch Road. If you've come up on route 1 you should turn off to the rhododendron reserve before continuing to Stewarts Point. The old general store here, built in 1868, is the only place on this trip—aside from Cazadero—where you can get food and drink.

From Stewarts Point the route back to Cazadero takes you through completely different country from what you've seen on your way up. Head inland on the Stewarts Point–Skaggs Springs Road, passing old farm buildings and at once entering a dark forest. The road climbs a bit, then twists down into the valley of the South Fork of the Gualala River. Here you are in the fault zone once again. You cross the river on an old steel bridge and climb steeply out of the valley. The road is one to one-and-a-half lanes, following the contour of the land and good for twenty to twenty-five mph —but there is little traffic. In a couple of miles you emerge from the forest and into sunlight, and in another mile or so you're at the Stewarts Point Indian Rancheria, home for fifteen or twenty families of Pomo Indians. Rancheria is a Spanish word that originally meant 'a collection of ranchos or rude dwellings.' In Spanish California it was applied to Indian villages in general.

Turn right onto Tin Barn Road. There is no name sign, but the turn is at the tall cylindrical water tower—just follow the yellow dashed line. The road runs along a ridge and is devoid of traffic. You pass an old farm situated in high meadows with grazing cattle—cattle that sometimes wander onto the road. Don't challenge them or drive rapidly at or past them, as they are easily frightened and usually make the wrong move—such as running directly in front of your car instead of away from it.

In about five miles is the junction with King Ridge Road, at a high point by a cluster of huge oaks. An attractive side trip from here is to take the right fork, Hauser Bridge Road. In about four miles this narrow road goes down a steep grade to cross the South Fork of the Gualala on a one-lane

Cazadero—Tin Barn

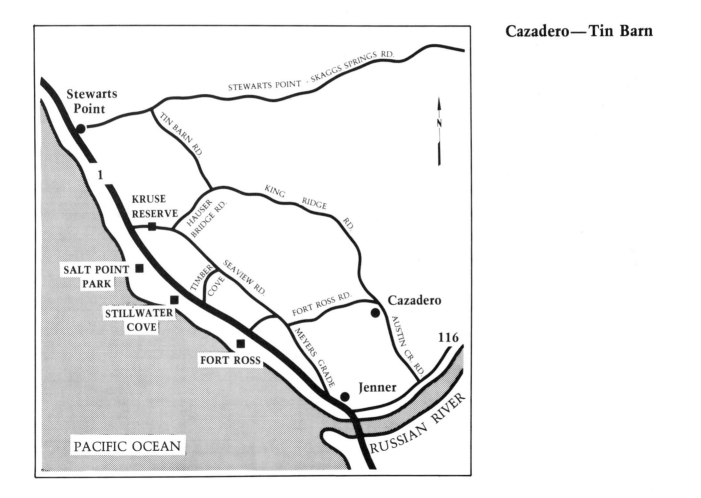

The Oredazac Oracle—
along the road to Cazadero,
where it got its name.

steel-honeycomb bridge, and up the other side (lots of wild iris in the spring) to Plantation—where you already may have been when headed north on the way to Stewarts Point. If you don't go to Plantation, at least go down to the bridge before retracing your steps to the junction by the cluster of oaks.

From the oaks it is seventeen miles to Cazadero on King Ridge Road. In many ways this is the best of all back roads. It's practically unspoiled country, most of it high meadows dotted with grazing sheep. There are wonderful views, an old abandoned schoolhouse shortly after leaving the junction, and several places where meandering and converging picket and split-rail fences seem to be arranged by an artistic hand rather than for a practical purpose. The first five and a half miles of the road from the junction are good-quality dirt, and it's paved after that. The dirt should be driven with care in wet weather.

King Ridge Road hits a high point of 1260 feet above sea level, before descending along Austin Creek where you can pick a spot for an informal picnic—or perhaps cool off in the water. All too soon you'll pass the junction of the Fort Ross Road—the route you took going north—and you'll be back in Cazadero. If you got here from the junction by the cluster of oaks in under an hour, you've been driving too fast.

Napa Valley-
Silverado Trail

The wineries of Napa Valley have been described, boosted, and extolled by the compilers of every guidebook on northern California for more than a century. The message has been conveyed so well that the wineries are thronged and the roads heavily traveled—not by people out for a leisurely tour but by those who drive as though in a great rush to get somewhere. But still, there are several interesting side trips leading out of Napa Valley, and since you have to go up the valley to reach them you might as well make the most of it.

State Route 29, the major north-south road in Napa Valley, should be avoided whenever possible. A better alternative for the entire distance from Napa to Calistoga is the Silverado Trail. This road also carries much traffic, but is preferable to route 29. As you reach the southern edge of Napa, where route 29 turns left, continue straight ahead on route 121 and follow the Silverado Trail signs. At the north edge of town you will go left on Trancas Street (a stop sign), then right on Silverado Trail.

The town of Napa had its beginning in 1848 when a Nathan Coombs erected the first building, a saloon. A two-story frame courthouse went up in 1850; Napa has always been the county seat of Napa County. Nine miles north of Napa on route 29 is the small community of Yountville, named for George C. Yount who came to California in 1831 with the William Wolfskill party. In 1836 Yount received a land grant of more than

11,000 acres in Napa Valley, and when he built his home it was the only white person's dwelling place inland between Sonoma and the Columbia River. Yount died in 1865 and is buried in the cemetery at the north end of town.

A recent development in Yountville would have stunned Mr. Yount: the conversion of some old brick winery buildings into a complex of specialty shops and eateries. The buildings are the former Groezinger Winery, in use from 1870 to 1954. Now they house what is called "Vintage 1870." There is an art gallery, bookstore, clothing and cookware shops, and a theater company, among other things. None of these will fit the budget of someone out for an inexpensive auto tour on back roads, but the complex is attractively done and it costs nothing to wander through. (Open 10 to 5; closed Mondays and major holidays.)

Yountville also has two old restored hotels—the Burgundy House, built in 1872 as a winery, and the Magnolia Hotel, built in 1873. They are expensive to stay in, but cost nothing to admire and photograph. There is a good public park at the north end of town, with picnic tables, restrooms, and plenty of green grass. If you are coming up the valley on Silverado Trail you reach Yountville by the Yountville Cross Road. If you're coming up route 29, take the Veterans Home turnoff and continue straight on up, parallel to 29. The Veterans Home is not quite as old as its oldest inhabitants, some of whom are over one hundred. It was opened in 1881 for disabled veterans of the Mexican War and the Grand Army of the Republic.

A much less traveled road goes from Napa up the west side of the valley for about half its length. From route 29 just north of Napa turn left on Redwood Road, and after a mile turn right on Dry Creek Road. The first mile or two are past old farms and modern subdivisions. The road soon narrows—and loses most of its traffic—as it winds along Dry Creek through madrone and oak trees. At the junction with Oakville Grade Road turn right, go uphill over a ridge, then steeply down the other side with great vistas across the valley. At the base of the hills, on your left, the Carmelite Monastery looks out across extensive vineyards. You meet route 29 at Oakville, three miles north of Yountville. Two tenths of a mile to the left on 29 is Oakville Cross Road, which leads to Silverado Trail. If you're going to visit Yountville, go right on 29 for one and a half miles and left on Yount Mill Road which brings you into town by the back way. You'll come

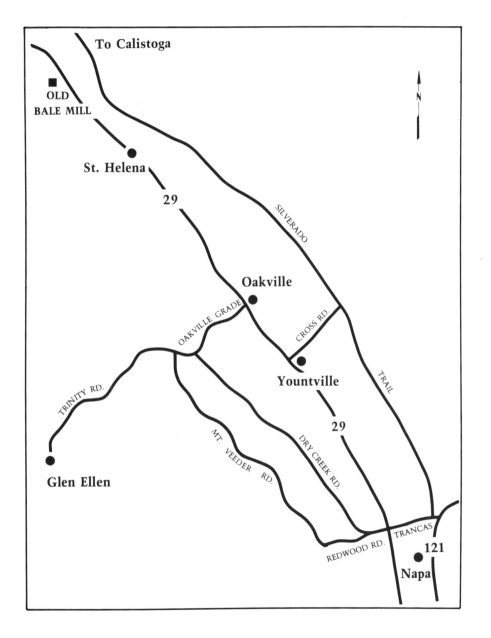

Napa—Silverado

in on Yount Street, which you follow down to its end where you turn right to Vintage 1870.

Continue up the valley past vineyards and orchards. Most of the major wineries are found along route 29 between Yountville and Calistoga. Not all have tours and tasting rooms, and the hours vary. In our opinion, the best guide to the wineries is the free pamphlet from the Wine Institute.

If you're on Silverado Trail as you near St. Helena, keep an eye out for Taplin Road, which turns off to the right about half a mile north of Zinfandel Lane. On the right is an old one-room schoolhouse that has been converted into a charming private home. Another mile and a half brings you to Pope Street where you turn left across a stone bridge—the oldest bridge in the county, built in 1894—and go into St. Helena. At the north end of town, just past the business district, is a picnic ground with tables. Turn right at the first street past the bandstand.

On this same street, Railroad Avenue, a couple of blocks back south, is the Silverado Museum, devoted to the life and works of Robert Louis Stevenson. The museum contains a private collection of Stevenson items: original manuscripts, first editions, letters, photographs, and memorabilia such as a writing desk, account book, and the toy lead soldiers Stevenson played with as a boy. (The museum is free, open to the public every day except Mondays and holidays from noon to 4.)

Three miles north of St. Helena on 29 is the Old Bale Mill, a state historic park. This was a gristmill built in 1846, with an overshot water wheel thirty-six feet in diameter. It contains much of the early equipment, and provides a fascinating look at the technology of the mid-nineteenth century. (The park is open daily from 9 to 4:30.) Unfortunately it is no longer possible to picnic in this attractive setting due to lack of space. Half a mile north of the old mill is Napa Valley State Park, which has picnic grounds and hiking trails. (Day use fee is $1.50.)

On Silverado Trail just before reaching Calistoga is the Calistoga Steam Railroad. The cars and locomotives are one-third scale, and operate over nearly three miles of track. They were originally used as an excursion railroad at the Panama Pacific International Exposition in San Francisco in 1915. (Summer schedule: 11 to 5, closed Mondays. Winter schedule: noon to 5, weather permitting, Saturday and Sunday only. Fares are: adults, $1.50; children under 12, $1.00; under 5, free.)

Calistoga was founded in 1859 by Samuel Brannan, who saw great possibilities in developing a resort based on the natural hot springs in the area. He built a hotel, twenty-five cottages, and a store. Legend has it that Brannan intended to make his spa the "Saratoga of California," but during his dedication speech he got his wires crossed and it came out as "the Calistoga of Sarafornia"—and Calistoga it is.

Brannan's old store is on Wapoo Street, a block off Lincoln Avenue, and is now a private home. The grounds of the original spa are now Pacheteau's Hot Springs, marked by a row of old palm trees, on Lincoln Avenue at the north end of town. One of the original cottages still exists. It has been moved into town and is being restored by the Napa County Historical Society.

A nice spot for a picnic is Pioneer Park. Go west from Lincoln Avenue on Cedar Street one block to Spring Street and turn right. The park is on the Napa River—hardly more than a creek—and is nicely shaded and secluded. There are tables, swings, slides, and restrooms.

Calistoga is still noted for its health spas, which offer mud and mineral baths and the accompanying massages and "chiropractic adjustments." A nineteenth-century writer described some of the health-spa clientele of his day: ". . . pale, feeble-looking ladies with bottles of medicine in their hands, and speaking to each other in subdued undertones, flitted noiselessly about, and tall, sallow-looking men, weak as children. . . ." Well, you don't *have* to be ill and weak to enjoy taking the waters. If you like that sort of thing, then here is the sort of thing you will like. The best source of information on the various spas, and on Calistoga and vicinity in general, is the Chamber of Commerce at 1316 Lincoln Avenue.

But all of this traveling on the well-trodden tourist paths, and visiting of the customary attractions, is merely to introduce you to Napa Valley and to orient you for the beginning of several back-roads tours that follow. When you are weary of too much traffic and too many other people, and your mind is befuddled by too much devotion to wine-tasting, you can escape to these remote country roads, and clear your head and lungs with that clean country air.

Mt. Veeder Road-Glen Ellen

You can spend the better part of a day going from Napa Valley to Sonoma Valley and on toward Santa Rosa, stopping along the way at a historic park dedicated to Jack London, the renowned California writer.

From State Route 29 just north of Napa, turn left on Redwood Road. In about two miles the road bends around to the northwest and ascends along Redwood Creek. Most of Napa Valley is flat, planted in vineyards and orchards, but here you are in a narrow valley between two rows of hills. At a fork in the road after several miles take the right fork, which is Mt. Veeder Road. This goes up through Pickle Canyon, where the branches of huge oaks, festooned with Spanish moss, hang over the road. You cross a low ridge and descend to meet Dry Creek Road—all of this takes approximately thirty to forty minutes of slow driving from Napa.

Turn left on Dry Creek Road, and check your odometer because it is four miles to the next turn, which is not marked. In a couple of miles you cross the high point, the Sonoma County line. The name changes to Trinity Road, and you start down at once toward Sonoma Valley. You will know your turn is coming up when you see a caution sign indicating a right-angle curve marked for ten miles per hour. Just at the head of the curve turn sharp left onto Cavedale Road.

This road bends around and follows near the ridge line for a couple of miles, then descends through dry, rocky hills while providing good views into the valley and beyond. Cavedale is a narrow road that follows the contours of the land, and when you get near the bottom there is a monument on the left that tells you why. In 1915 the local residents apparently were unable to persuade the county to build a road where they thought one should be. So they built their own road, financing it with public donations. Two donors contributed the right of way, and others chipped in amounts that ranged from $5 to $165. Not far past the monument is the junction with State Route 12. Turn right here and go for about half a mile, then turn left on Madrone Road. In one mile you'll come to Arnold Drive where you turn right and go two miles to Glen Ellen.

Glen Ellen was named in 1869 by Charles V. Stuart, a Pennsylvanian and 1849 pioneer, for his wife Ellen Mary. The town is at the northern end of Sonoma Valley, which Jack London made famous by giving it the romantic name of "Valley of the Moon." It's not certain how London came up with the name. The valley is said to have been called "Valle de la Luna" as long ago as the 1840s. But perhaps London simply chose to ignore what one authority says about the name Sonoma: it's derived from an Indian word meaning 'nose,' which is presumed to come either from a geologic feature or from an Indian chief with a prominent snout. But "Big Nose Valley" is somewhat lacking in poetry.

As you bear left up the hill on London Ranch Road, the state park entrance is about a mile. London came to this ranch in 1905, and lived here until his death in 1916 at the age of forty. A short walk from the parking lot brings you to the "House of Happy Walls," built between 1919 and 1922 by London's widow, Charmian, who lived here until her death in 1955. It is constructed of native fieldstone, with a Spanish-style tiled roof, and is now a museum displaying a collection of London's manuscripts, photographs, and the artifacts collected during his travels in the South Seas. A library has been furnished with items from London's study: his rolltop desk, a dictaphone, and pictures that show him at work on his writing. The house is well maintained by the state, and the fifty-cent admission charge is a bargain. (The hours are 10 to 5, open daily except Thanksgiving, Christmas, and New Year's Day.)

Take the time and energy to make an easy one-mile round trip walk to Wolf House, the magnificent ruins of Jack London's house—a place that was never inhabited. It was built between 1910 and 1913, using native materials, at a cost of approximately $80,000—which at present values

Mt. Veeder—Glen Ellen

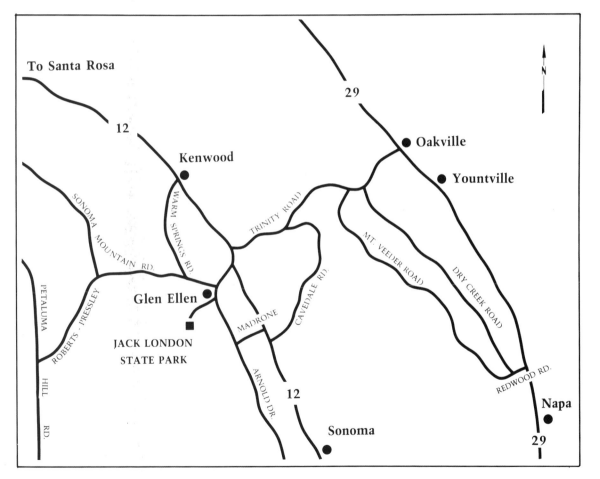

*Jack London's Wolf House—
the stone walls were built to
last forever but the house
itself was never inhabited.*

would be close to $1 million. The house was done on the grand scale: a two-story-high living room with an immense fireplace; a dining room that could seat fifty people; numerous guest rooms; a fireproof vault in the basement to protect London's manuscripts and other valuable possessions. Just before the Londons were going to move into the house, it was destroyed by fire. The stone walls, archways, and chimneys still stand, looking much as they did just after the fire. On the way to the Wolf House, a short side trail takes you to Jack London's grave under a rough, unmarked boulder.

Return to Glen Ellen, turn left on Arnold Drive, and very shortly turn left on Warm Springs Road. This snakes through dark woods and around hills for four or five miles. Turn left on Pressley Road, which crosses a low ridge through grazing land, changes its name to Roberts Road, and goes down to meet Petaluma Hill Road. At this junction turn right for Santa Rosa and U.S. 101 north, or left to Petaluma and U.S. 101 south.

Pope Valley-Aetna Springs

There are several loop trips that will take you away from the crush of traffic in Napa Valley. These can be made easily in half a day, or can even be stretched into a full day if you include a picnic and don't try to break any speed records. All of these get you into higher, open country, with excellent distant views of the surrounding hills and across grazing lands—a terrain quite different from the towns and vineyards of the valley.

From Rutherford, four miles south of St. Helena, take State Route 128 east toward Lake Berryessa. There may be considerable traffic at the beginning of this trip, but only for a few miles. The road follows along the shore of Lake Hennessy, and though the lake invites a picnic or swimming, these are not allowed. The lake is a municipal water supply, and the only permissible activity is fishing—and even that requires a permit.

At the end of the lake take the Chiles and Pope Valley Road to the left, leaving behind most of the traffic which continues on to Lake Berryessa. The road winds up a narrow, shallow gorge beside a stream bed, and then opens into a valley. Several miles farther on you climb over a low ridge and quickly descend into Pope Valley which is some 500 feet higher than Napa Valley. If you are here on a weekend in fair weather, as we were, keep an eye on the sky to your right as you go down the grade and you may be lucky enough to see large spots of bright color floating against the blue. Parachutists and sky-divers practice here, operating out of the Pope Valley Parachute Ranch. Turn right on Pope Canyon Road at the foot of the grade, and you'll be at the ranch in a mile. The sky-divers wear colorful outfits to increase their visibility. Before going up, they practice the formations and movements they will perform while free-falling.

From the intersection at the Parachute Ranch take Pope Valley Middle Road. In a mile turn right at the stop sign, and in another mile you're at the hamlet of Pope Valley. The town, valley, and creek were named for William Pope, who came to California with the James Ohio Pattie party in 1828—the second group of Americans to arrive via an overland route.

Turn right and go on up the valley. At about two miles keep an eye out for a road going left. This is Ink Grade Road, your return route, and it isn't well marked. Go on past it another mile to Litto's, a place so glaringly obvious it will almost knock your eyes out. Here is 'hubcap art' developed to the highest degree. The house, driveway, fences, and fenceposts are festooned with a glittering array of chrome hubcaps, pastel-painted tires, flattened cans, miniature figures, and the sort of trinkets that graced mantelpieces fifty years ago.

A mile past Litto's turn left on an unmarked road just before the road you're on makes a sharp bend to the right. One mile up this road brings you to Aetna Springs, a former resort. It's private property now, not open to the public. But though you can't get into the grounds, most of the layout is easily seen from the road. The major buildings look as though they date from the turn of the century or before. There is a stone gateway and extensive stone fences and the entire area is in deep shade. It's like having gone through a time warp to come upon this relic of another age.

Return to Pope Valley Road and turn right. (If you're headed for the vicinity of Clear Lake, turning left takes you to Middletown and a junction with State Route 29 in about 15 miles.) Go past Litto's again—if the sight doesn't blind you—and turn right on Ink Grade Road. It's the only paved side road in this stretch, so start up it with confidence even if you don't see a sign. It's narrow and winding through thick woods, and though traffic is negligible you should be cautious on sharp, blind curves.

Turn right on White Cottage Road—the first stop sign—and angle right at a three-way intersection a mile farther on. A couple of more miles from that intersection is another stop sign, the main road between Pope Valley and St. Helena. Go straight across—with caution, as it's difficult to see well in either direction—and continue downhill on Howell Mountain Road with fine views into Conn Valley to the southeast. Four or five miles of winding around curves brings you back to a junction with the Silverado Trail close to Pope Street bridge on the outskirts of St. Helena. And you're right back in Napa Valley, where you began. If you didn't come back this way, then you're somewhere else.

Pope Valley

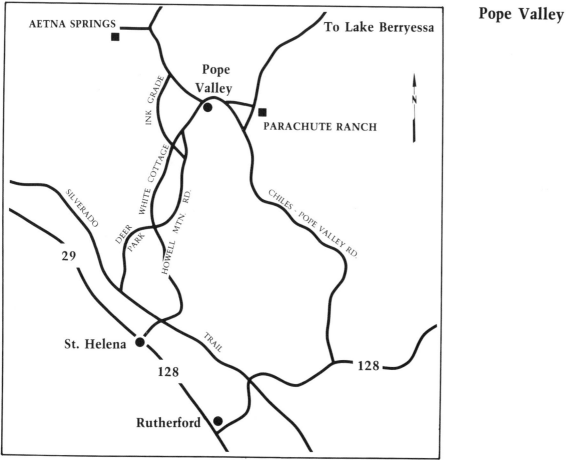

Mark West Springs-
Petrified Forest

North of Napa Valley—with its towns, extensive vineyards, and active commercial life—is Knights Valley. Although it is only two hundred feet higher than Napa Valley, the terrain is noticeably different. There are occasional small knolls, and some pine trees on the valley floor. The most obvious difference is the relative absence of human intervention. Cattle grazing is the predominant activity. There are no vineyards or orchards, and nary a housing tract to be seen.

Go north from Calistoga on route 128. In about four miles you pass over a low divide, cross into Sonoma County, and descend to Knights Valley. The low divide is also a watershed. The land south of it is drained by the Napa River, which flows south to San Pablo Bay. The various streams in Knights Valley flow into the Russian River, which runs generally westward to the ocean.

As you might have suspected, the valley was named for an early settler, a Thomas Knight who came here in the 1850s. William H. Brewer came through Knights Valley in November, 1861, with a surveying party, and though he does not mention Mr. Knight, the valley was already known by that name. He does refer to a man named McDonald (whose name remains on a nearby creek), and characterizes him as "a quiet, fine man, and what is rare in such regions, a pious man. He settled here twelve or fifteen years ago, then the remotest settler in this region between San Francisco and the settlements in Oregon." How settled and tamed most of this country is today, yet its "civilized" history began just one hundred thirty-five years ago—a mere four or five generations.

About three miles north of the county line, turn left on Franz Valley Road. Even on a sunny weekend, when it seems as if the entire population of the state is out for a drive, this road is almost deserted. Along Franz Creek you will see an occasional fisherman, but this road isn't used by the high-speed crowd—those going from here to there as quickly as possible. At five miles you climb away from the creek—along which the resourceful will find places to picnic—and pass the junction of Franz Valley School Road, which turns off left and returns to Calistoga. Franz Valley Road narrows, loses its center line—a sure indication of a lightly used road—crosses over a ridge and goes steeply down the other side. Stop along the downgrade and enjoy a long view straight ahead to the southwest and down Porter Creek Valley to the left. As you will see, the Porter Creek Road is where the traffic is, and you will have to go down to join the procession—though on weekdays the traffic is light.

Turn right at the stop sign and go two miles to Mark West Springs. This was once a famous spa, and a stage stop between San Francisco and the northwest, and is the oldest functioning resort in California. The hot springs and the baths are no more, nor are there accommodations for overnight guests. But the lodge serves expensive French cuisine, claimed by the proprietors to be "the best in America." (Open March 1 to Thanksgiving, daily except Wednesday from 5:30 to 10; Sunday, 4 to 9. The bar opens at 5 on weekdays and 2 on Sunday, so you can enjoy an aperitif while awaiting dinner. For reservations, phone (707) 546-2592.) The lodge fronts directly on the road, and the one remnant from its earliest days is an enormous grapevine that carries clear across the road on a wooden framework.

If you continue on past Mark West Lodge for seven miles you will come to U.S. 101 five miles north of Santa Rosa. However, there is more to be seen en route back to Calistoga. Return the way you came, go right on Porter Creek Road, left at the next junction, and one more mile to the Petrified Forest on the left.

The forest is an area a mile long and a quarter of a mile wide of petrified redwoods. The first excavations were begun in 1871 by Charles Evans (who, naturally, acquired the nickname "Petrified Charlie"), a prospector and homesteader. He removed the brush and overburden from the fallen trees, put up a fence, and charged admission—the traditional reaction of someone who has stumbled upon a natural wonder. After his death the land was used agriculturally until 1914, when a new owner took over and did extensive excavation and development. The largest trees yet uncovered are the "Queen of the Forest," 80 feet long and 12 feet in circumference, and "The Monarch," 126 feet long and 4 feet in diameter. There are also marine fossils and fossilized leaves. The trees lie in two tiers, with their tips pointing away from Mount St. Helena, indicating that lava flows from that peak overwhelmed the forest millions of years ago—the agent that killed the trees was also the one that preserved them. The preservation has been so perfect that the smallest fiber and texture remain intact, but as mineral rather than wood.

Robert Louis Stevenson visited the Petrified Forest in 1880, and called it "a pure little isle of touristy among these solitary hills." He seems to have enjoyed the company of the proprietor, but was considerably less than enthralled by the forest itself. "It is very curious, of course, and ancient enough, if that were all. Doubtless, the heart of the geologist beats quicker at the sight; but, for my part, I was mightily unmoved. Sightseeing is the art of disappointment."

But surely it's a matter of individual preference. If you feel interested, then pay the $1.50 admission and go right in; children under 10 get in free. There is a free picnic ground adjacent to the parking area. Calistoga is but four miles away, and completes the loop. (For the map to this trip, see p. 63.)

Silverado Mine-
Great Western Mine Road

Robert Louis Stevenson on his way up the stage road from Calistoga to Mount St. Helena:

> Vineyards and deep meadows, islanded and framed with thicket, gave place more and more as we ascended to woods of oak and madrona, dotted with enormous pines. . . . A rough smack of resin was in the air, and a crystal mountain purity. It came pouring over these green slopes by the oceanful. . . . There are days in a life when thus to climb out of the lowlands, seems like scaling heaven.

The modern traveler can follow much the same route today, and in nine miles be within a mile of the site of the old cabin where Stevenson and his bride Fanny spent three weeks during the spring of 1880. The way to what is now Robert Louis Stevenson State Park is via State Route 29 north from Calistoga. This is the major road to Clear Lake, and there is more traffic on it than one would like. Nevertheless, you can drive up the grade at a moderate pace. There are several long stretches with passing lanes, and traffic of all speeds is easily accommodated. There are numerous places where you might wish to pull off to enjoy the view back down the valley and ahead up the road to the rocky crags of the Mayacmas Mountains.

Route 29 is the fast and common way of getting up the hill. The slower and uncommon way, which we much prefer, is via Lawley Road, which follows the route of the old toll road. Lawley Road turns right off of route 29 in the middle of a vineyard about one and a half miles north of the junction of 29 and Silverado Trail. The sign says both Old Toll Road and Lawley Road. It's paved all the way up, but the major part of it is only one lane wide. (A note of caution: this road is definitely not suitable for recreational vehicles or for cars pulling trailers.) On the one-lane portions, remember the rule of the road: uphill traffic has the right of way—though if you meet someone, courtesy and common sense will dictate who should back up. The road winds steeply up along a hillside, offering fine views of the mountains as you get higher, and passing a couple of old farms. When you come to route 29 turn right up the hill, and it's only about two miles to the summit.

There are days in winter and spring when a heavy fog lies in the valley, making the world gray and gloomy. But often you will find, as you drive toward Mount St. Helena, that halfway up you'll break out above the fog and be under a blue sky, looking down on the tops of hills poking through the covering of white.

Stevenson State Park is undeveloped, but provides opportunities for some easy hiking. Just as you reach the summit there are parking areas on both sides of the road. A fire trail leads north, away from the highway. The remnants of the old Toll House foundations can be seen, and there are a few picnic tables on the flat above the road. In half a mile you come to "a canyon, woody below, red, rocky, and naked overhead. . . ." (This and the other quotes in this section are from Stevenson's *The Silverado Squatters*.) It was here that an iron chute brought ore from the Silverado Mine and dumped it into the canyon, from which it was carried away by carts to a mill.

Half a mile farther you are at a "triangular platform, filling up the whole glen, and shut in on either hand by bold projections of the mountain. Only in front the place was open like the proscenium of a theatre. . . ." In 1880 the remnants of the mining activity were still much in evidence: iron rails, old wood, a blacksmith's forge, and the old wooden house where Louis and Fanny lived. All of this has long since disappeared, and in their place is the Stevenson Monument: an open book carved from polished granite and mounted on a base of ore from the mine. From this place you can gaze out,

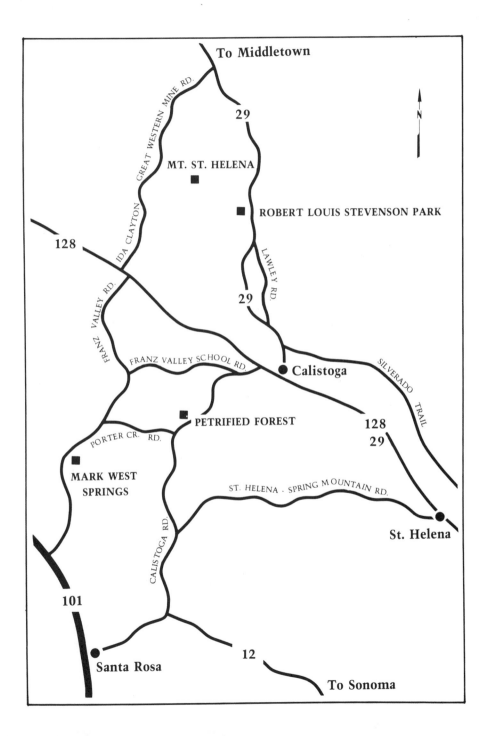

**Mark West Springs—
Great Western Mine Road**

as Stevenson did, "into a great realm of air, and down upon treetops and hilltops, and far and near on wild and varied country."

Even then, nearly a century ago, California had a fine collection of ghost towns. "Already there have been many cycles of population succeeding each other, and passing away and leaving behind them relics. The towns . . . are experimentally founded: they grow great and prosper by passing occasions; and when the lode comes to an end, and the miners move elsewhere, the town remains behind them, like Palmyra in the desert." From the site of the Silverado Mine you can continue four miles on up the fire trail to the top of Mount St. Helena. But it will be more strenuous than the easy hike thus far: the altitude gain from where you parked your car to the summit is 1400 feet.

Route 29 descends toward Middletown, and soon crosses into Lake County. About six miles from the summit turn left on the Great Western Mine Road. It's narrow and winding, but don't be put off—it's perfectly good for any sort of passenger car, though not for recreational vehicles and trailers. The first mile is paved, then there is a good gravel surface to the summit at the Sonoma County line. Fifteen to twenty miles per hour is all this road is good for.

About two miles along you will see some buildings in an open area downhill from the road. This was the former Great Western Quicksilver Mine, which produced continuously from 1873 to 1909. There has been some mining since that time, but nothing on a large scale, and though the property appears to be inhabited it is doubtful that any mining is taking place. There is a highly informative, entertaining, and moving book about the Great Western, written by a woman whose father was superintendent of the mine from 1876 to 1900: *The Life and Death of a Quicksilver Mine*, by Helen Rocca Goss.

At the summit, where you come onto pavement again, is a grand spot for a picnic, with a fine prospect of country to the south and west. From this point on, the road is called the Ida Clayton Road. It's paved all the way down, but is only a lane and a half wide and requires caution on the blind curves. With any luck you won't meet a single vehicle on the entire 12-mile stretch from route 29 to the junction of route 128. There are many good picnic spots, all of them offering views into Alexander Valley—where the Russian River flows—and of the rugged west side of Mount St. Helena.

From the upper part of the descent you can see, to the northwest, several spurts of steam from The Geysers.

There is some disagreement as to how the mountain acquired its name. Russians from the settlement at Fort Ross made the first known ascent, in 1841. One of the climbers was supposed to have been a Princess Helena de Gagarin, a niece of the Czar, and the peak was named after St. Helena, her patron saint. Another possibility is that it was named by the Russians from a ship at sea, as it is the highest peak in this latitude and is visible from seventy-five miles at sea. The town of St. Helena was so named because it commands a good view of the mountain.

The Ida Clayton Road is so attractive, and so seldom traveled, that you may be inclined to spend the day lazing in the sun. When you do get down to the junction with route 128, going left gets you back to Calistoga and going right takes you to Alexander Valley and the road to The Geysers. If you want to do this trip in reverse, or use the Ida Clayton Road–Western Mine Road portion as an alternative route from Calistoga to Middletown and Clear Lake, you'll have to be alert to find the beginning of Ida Clayton Road. About eight miles north of Calistoga on route 128 you will cross Redwood Creek. Ida Clayton Road turns off to the right about one hundred yards past the creek.

The Geysers

The Geysers were known to the Indians long before white people arrived in California, and were used for essentially the same purpose to which the whites later put them: healing the sick with medicinal waters. A guidebook published in 1881 states that there was "a jet called the Indian sweatbath, where the rheumatic patient was wont to be brought and laid upon the scaffold, or temporary grating, immediately over the spring, and steamed until cured or relieved by death from his sufferings."

The compiler of the guidebook does not say how he came by his information; it is doubtful that he witnessed the parboiling of Indians. William B. Elliott, a hunter and trapper, the first white man to see The Geysers, came upon them in 1847 while chasing a bear. Naturally he returned with the report that he had discovered the gates of hell, and soon the more prominent features at The Geysers had acquired such names as "The Devil's Machine Shop," "Witches' Cauldron." and "Proserpine's Grotto." By the late 1850s there was a hotel at The Geysers, and in 1861 the first buggy reached the locale over a newly-built wagon road. This road has not been used for a century. The present roads, from Alexander Valley and from Cloverdale, were built as toll roads in 1869 and 1874 respectively.

Start at the junction at Jim Town on route 128, sixteen miles north of Calistoga and eight miles south of Geyserville. About two miles north of Jim Town, Geysers Road turns off to the right. (Midway in this two-mile stretch is Honey Dew Acres, a place on the west side of the road where excellent honey is sold. The house number is 5155; look for the Farm Trails sign.) The Geysers Road winds uphill through oak, madrone, and manzanita, but in a few miles breaks out into the open. Cattle graze on the hills, there are occasional rocky outcroppings and clumps of oaks, and you have grand views in all directions. This is another of those routes that might be just the thing for escaping the gloom of a foggy day in the valleys: most of it is above one thousand feet altitude, and thus—hopefully—above the fog. If you plan a picnic lunch somewhere, it is best to have it on this uphill part of the trip where there are many attractive places. The return portion—the road to Cloverdale—follows along the canyon of Big Sulphur Creek where it is not easy to find a suitable spot.

The word "geysers" is actually a misnomer, so don't expect to see spouts of water like Old Faithful in Yellowstone. The most spectacular features are spouts of steam, but the most common ones—though not so visible—are springs of boiling, bubbling water. If the wind is wrong, there is the unmistakable odor of hydrogen sulphide—rotten eggs.

At the road junction turn right, upstream, and in a short distance is a viewpoint with three plaques describing the geologic origin of The Geysers and their present use by Union Oil Company of California to produce steam, which is utilized by Pacific Gas and Electric Company to generate electricity. This is the only geothermal power plant in the United States, and by far the largest in the world. By the end of 1979, PG & E will be generating 908,000 kilowatts of electricity at The Geysers. Though it is not possible to predict the ultimate capacity, developers of the field believe it could be as great as two million kilowatts.

From the viewpoint, continue to the end of the road at a cluster of buildings, including a cafe. It is possible to buy a permit here, for a dollar, and drive up about another mile. We didn't do this, as we suspected it would be money ill spent: you won't see any more, or anything better, than you've already seen. There no longer is a functioning resort. The major business of the cafe seems to be selling six-packs of beer to the men who work up here and commute from the valley. We strongly recommend that you not be on the road while these bravados are whipping their steeds around the curves during the afternoon commute.

Foss, the famous stage-driver, originated and owned the line between Calistoga and The Geysers in the 1870s and 1880s. He had a reputation for

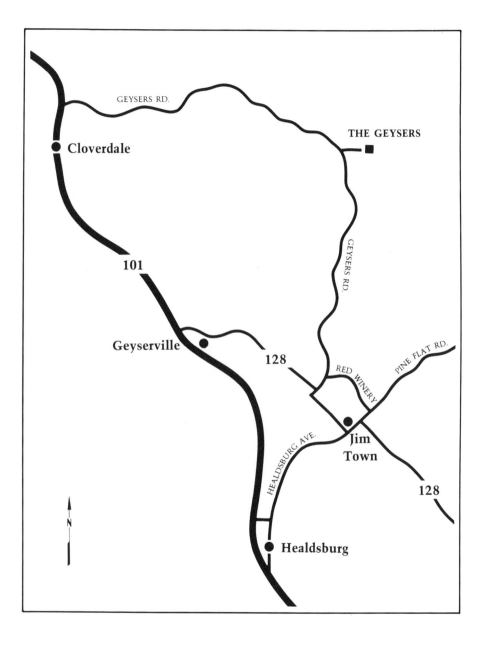

The Geysers

GEYSERS RD.

THE GEYSERS

● Cloverdale

101

GEYSERS RD.

Geyserville ●

128

RED WINERY

PINE FLAT RD.

HEALDSBURG AVE.

Jim
Town

128

N

● Healdsburg

Geysers Road follows the route of an old toll road that was built in 1869.

great skill and strength, and a penchant for running a stage full tilt on the downgrades. An early traveler described a downhill run with Foss:

> Trees fly past like the wind; bushes dash angrily against the wheels; . . . and we speed down the declivity with lightning rapidity, the horses on a live jump, and General Foss, whip in hand, cracking it above their heads to urge them on. . . . At every lurch of the coach one feels an instinctive dread of being tossed high in the air and landed far below—in a gorge, or perchance spitted upon the top of a sharp pine. If a horse should stumble or misstep, or the tackle snap, away we should all go down a precipice. The angle of descent is exceedingly sharp, and down this declivity the horses are run at break-neck speed for two and a half miles, making thirty-five turns. . . .

Return to the junction and take the right fork down Big Sulphur Creek toward Cloverdale, sixteen miles away. This road is less modern than the one you came up: narrower, and with sharper curves. By way of compensation, there is very little traffic. It's difficult to pass, and if someone faster should catch up to you, look for a wide spot so you can pull over and let him by. The scenery is different, too. Rather than being on rolling uplands you are following along a fairly deep canyon, sometimes almost down to stream level and at others high on the slope above. At the junction with U.S. 101, Cloverdale is two miles to the left, and Santa Rosa is thirty-two miles.

Chalk Hill Road-
Pine Flat Road

California seems to provide the right atmosphere for the growth of the new, the experimental, and the bizarre. The forerunners of today's communes and religious retreats flourished briefly in the nineteenth century, usually in the form of utopian colonies that offered their members a release from worldly cares—plus the promise of considerable spiritual and physical benefit. One of the more noted—or notorious—of these was the Brotherhood of New Life, whose spiritualist leader, Thomas Lake Harris, modestly took the title of "Primate and King."

In the 1870s Harris bought 1500 acres of land just north of Santa Rosa, and established his new Eden. The faithful were engaged in living a blend of mysticism, socialism (they had to give all their possessions to the organization), and a search for their spiritual mates—which may not have been your husband or wife, meaning that you had to keep looking. (If this sounds as though it just happened during the past ten years, it simply proves that there is nothing new under the sun.) Naturally the good people of Santa Rosa thought this practice amounted to "free love"—than which there was nothing worse. To support themselves the colonists planted vineyards, and for many years after the colony collapsed, the Fountain Grove Winery produced excellent wines.

As you go north on U.S. 101 past Santa Rosa, take the Mendocino Avenue exit at the north edge of the city. One of the early buildings from the colony, a round barn bearing a Fountain Grove Winery sign, sits prominently on a hill to your right.

From the freeway exit continue north on Old Redwood Highway, which was U.S. 101 before the freeway was built. Soon you come to Mark West Springs Road (a traffic light), and about a mile beyond that you should angle right on Faught Road. This road narrows and loses its center line, and gets out of the built-up area along the old highway. You coast along close to the base of the hills, passing new, producing, and abandoned vineyards, with a view to the left across a broad valley to the Russian River. Keep right on Faught Road where E. Shiloh Road goes straight, and right again on Chalk Hill Road a mile farther on. In three miles you'll pass Chalk Hill, on the left, a knob that has earned a name by virtue of being a few feet higher than the other local knobs.

As you pass over a low ridge you'll have a sudden view of Mount St. Helena, and then the road runs along a wide valley with a rocky stream bed. Most of the terrain is grassy hills with scattered live oaks, but occasional coniferous trees give it a more northerly aspect.

Turn left at the junction of State Route 128, and in two and a half miles you'll come to Johnson's Alexander Valley Winery on the left. The tasting room and some picnic tables are at the end of a long lane. When you go in the visitors entrance you will find yourself among the aging tanks—an unusual introduction—and the tasting room has an organ, which gets played one Sunday a month. There are fresh pears available in August. (Open daily, 10 to 5.)

From the winery continue north on 128, and in just under two miles turn right on Pine Flat Road where 128 goes left. At the next junction the route to The Geysers goes left, but you keep straight on. Pine Flat Road becomes narrow at once, just as you pass some old farm buildings. There is an outside chance of meeting a big truck on this road, so keep to the right on the curves. For a while there is a creek on your left, but the road soon climbs along the hillsides and gets into more open country with tremendous views. Several miles along will find you on the pine flat that probably accounts for the name. For a stretch you will be crossing a broad upland meadow with a meandering stream. It looks much like a glaciated valley misplaced from some mountainous region. There are innumerable picnic spots along the way, and since you have to return by this same road you might pick out a choice one and come back to it later.

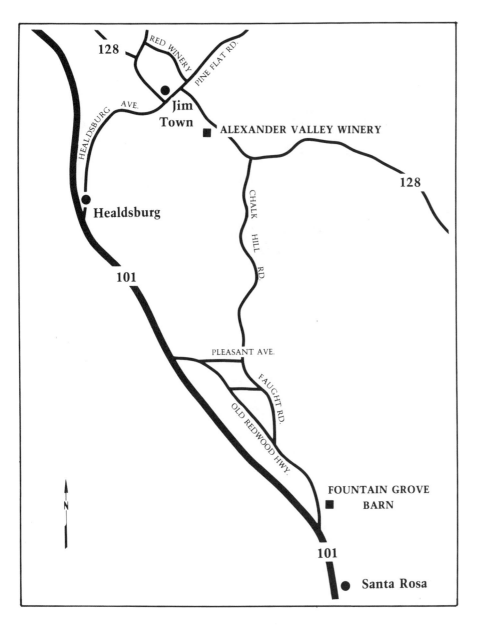

Chalk Hill—Pine Flat

128

RED WINERY

PINE FLAT RD.

HEALDSBURG AVE.

Jim
Town

■ **ALEXANDER VALLEY WINERY**

128

Healdsburg

CHALK HILL RD.

101

PLEASANT AVE.

FAUGHT RD.

OLD REDWOOD HWY.

FOUNTAIN GROVE
■ BARN

101

● Santa Rosa

N

Water towers are a vanishing breed. They are built of wood and held together with cables.

The road climbs again to an old mining area, in dry hills with scrub brush, digger pine, and manzanita. A herd of domestic goats grazes among the mine ruins and clambers onto old machinery. Ahead, on the ridge line, you may see a huge drilling rig. In the spring of 1978 Gulf Oil began drilling here—not for oil, but for steam. You are only about four crow-fly miles from The Geysers. If Gulf is successful there may be more drilling, and construction—hence the warning about possible truck traffic. The old mine might be a good place to turn around and head back down. This is a county road that is in good shape, however, so you may want to drive on up to the ridge—another two miles.

When you have returned to the valley continue straight to Jim Town, where you turn right on 128 if you're headed for The Geysers (see The Geysers trip) or to Geyserville and access to U.S. 101 north. Going to the left on 128, back the way you came, takes you to Calistoga and Napa Valley. If you want to get onto 101 headed south, go straight past Jim Town on Alexander Valley Road. In a couple of miles turn left on Healdsburg Avenue. Soon you come to the Simi Winery on the right. (There are picnic tables, and a tasting room open daily 10 to 5; closed on major holidays.) In another mile you can turn right to get to 101, or go straight another mile into Healdsburg where you can also get onto 101.

Briones
and the Muir House

Less than an hour's drive from anywhere in the Bay Area, a combination of topography and historical accident has preserved a park of rolling hills and thickly wooded stream beds in Contra Costa County. Briones Regional Park, but a few miles from freeways in all directions, is part of the East Bay Municipal Utility District's watershed, encompassing the high ground at the head of Pinole Creek.

A large area, which included the present park, was granted in 1823 to Ignacio Martinez, *commandante* at the San Francisco Presidio, as a reward for his military services. Martinez, in turn, permitted Felipe Briones, a soldier at the Presidio, to settle on the land in 1829. Briones had a ranch of more than 13,000 acres, but despite the size of his home territory he managed to roam too far afield. In 1840 he was killed while chasing Indians near Clayton.

Although Briones Park is well known to local people, and given moderate use on weekends, it never seems to be overcrowded. On weekdays it is semi-deserted, and if you walk more than a mile from the parking lot you will be alone—except, perhaps, for the cattle that graze the hills and are quite leery of any human presence.

You reach Briones by turning off Freeway 24 at Orinda. Go two miles north on Camino Pablo (San Pablo Dam Road) to Bear Valley Road, where you turn right, climb past the dam that has created Briones Reservoir, and in just over four miles come to the entrance to the park. An alternate route, if you are in Berkeley or the vicinity, is via Wildcat Canyon Road through Tilden Park. Bear Valley Road is simply straight ahead from where Wildcat Canyon Road meets San Pablo Dam Road.

Several trails begin at the parking lot, where trail maps are available. (Parking costs $2.00 on weekends, $1.00 on weekdays.) If you want to give your legs and lungs a good workout you can head for Briones Peak, the highest spot in the park at 1483 feet, from which there is a grand view of a country that appears almost uninhabited—except in the direction of Martinez. Adjacent to the parking lot is a large well-shaded picnic ground that will be comfortable on even the hottest days. There is ample space for children to burn up energy while the adults lounge in the shade.

Bear Creek Road north from Briones soon changes to a narrower surface and winds along Pinole Creek past several farms to the junction of Alhambra Valley Road. Turn right here, and meander along a road made to order for a leisurely drive—it rises gradually up to a low summit, then gradually descends past a pig farm and along Arroyo del Hambre. In about four and a half miles you come to the northern entrance to Briones Park. Drive a mile and a half up a paved road to its end. There is no organized picnic ground or other facilities here, as this is primarily a starting point for trails connecting with those from the Bear Valley entrance, but it's worth driving up the road for the view.

Alhambra Valley Road turns left a short distance beyond the park entrance. One and a half miles north, just past the John Muir Parkway (State Route 4), is the John Muir House—a fitting place to end after having enjoyed a drive through the countryside. Muir was the nation's foremost conservationist, and did more than anyone else to create our system of national parks and forests.

The house, on a knoll with a commanding view of the surrounding country, was Muir's residence from 1890 until his death in 1914. It is now under the protection of the National Park Service. (The house is open every day from 8:30 to 4:30, except Thanksgiving, Christmas, and New Year's Day. Admission is 50 cents; free for those under 12 and over 65.) A film on Muir is shown on the hour, and there also is a film on Ishi at 11 and 3:30. After the film you may stroll through the several acres of restored orchards and vineyards that give a fair idea of what this 2,600-acre ranch once was like. You soon become oblivious of the nearby freeway, business places, and houses, and appreciate the beauty and tranquillity of a rural

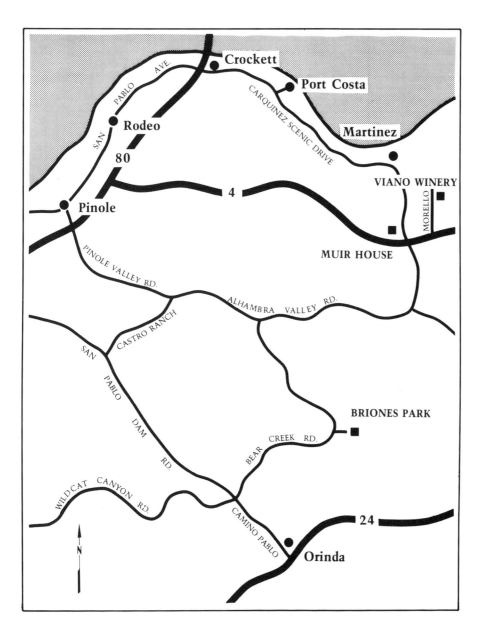

Briones and Port Costa

Parts of Briones Regional Park and the surrounding countryside are still devoted to cattle-grazing.

setting preserved from an unhurried age.

Tours of the house are self-guided. Muir's study has his rolltop desk, his papers and books and artifacts. There's a piano in the parlor, and a lovely table and sideboard in the dining room. The kitchen implements are in place, and in the attic you'll find the sorts of things that people usually put in attics. It almost seems as though the occupants are away for a time, and will soon return to take up their lives again.

Past the orchard, at the west end of the grounds, is the Vicente Martinez Adobe, built in 1849. It is not yet fully restored or furnished. (At present it is open to the public only from 1 to 4 on Sundays.) Behind the house is a shaded picnic area with two tables and barbecue pits—a choice spot for lunch.

If you wish to extend this off-the-beaten-path day, and have developed a thirst, get onto the route 4 freeway and go east one and a quarter miles to the Morello Avenue exit. North on Morello about a mile is the Conrad Viano Winery—some pink buildings on the right side just before the railroad trestle. (Open 9 to 12 and 1 to 5.) The basement of the family home serves as an informal tasting room and sales department. Viano has red, white, and dessert wines—also fresh apricots in season and often dried apricots at other times. Along with a glass of wine you'll get hospitality and conversation, and you can buy a bottle of your palate's desire and picnic beside the vineyard.

Carquinez
Scenic Drive-
Port Costa-Crockett

Carquinez Strait, the exit for the waters of the Sacramento and San Joaquin Rivers, was discovered by the Fages Expedition in 1772. The first name given to the strait was *Boca del Puerto Dulce*—mouth of the fresh-water port. Carquinez is derived from the Karquin Indians, and the name was spelled with a *K* until early in this century. A visitor to California in the gold rush days compared the strait to the Bosporus, but said that the bays and headlands of its "bold shores" gave Carquinez a greater natural beauty.

The Carquinez Scenic Drive begins at the northwest corner of Martinez. Take the Alhambra Avenue exit from Route 4 freeway, go north to Escobar Street (stop sign), left three blocks to Talbart Street, and right three blocks to the beginning of the drive. (Uphill to the left in this second three-block stretch is a municipal park with picnic tables.)

The road winds around steep hillsides, ducking into a hollow and coming out again around a knob, presenting an ever-changing view across Carquinez Strait and east to Suisun Bay and up the Sacramento River. In just a mile or so you will see the Benicia-Martinez Bridge from an unusual angle. Directly below the road, almost at water level, are the Southern Pacific Railroad tracks. There are occasional turnouts where you can stop to enjoy the view or to snap a photo.

In about four miles the road bends inland, and soon comes to the turnoff to Port Costa. As you get close to the business district there are, on the right, two remarkable examples of the "wood-butchers" art: two-story, hand-built, redwood houses, with outside stairways and a few stained glass windows. The first of these is on Canyon Lake Drive, the main street. The second is one block uphill at the Doll House Museum. It has high gables and looks like something out of nineteenth century England: vaguely sinister, perhaps the perfect setting for a horror film.

The Doll House Museum contains an intriguing collection of old dolls and toys. Among the unusual items are what is claimed to be the first music box made in the United States, and a replica of "The Last Supper" painted on a pinhead. (The museum is open daily 10 to 7; closed Monday. Admission is $1.00 for adults, 25¢ for children under 12.)

The block-long business district, which had declined to a state of semi-abandonment, has been revived in recent years. On the right hand side is the Warehouse, home for a cafe and more than twenty shops offering antiques, furniture, jewelry, coins, and—to cover everything—collectibles. One shop is called Treasures and Trivia, which competes with Ellen's Closet and Oliver's Oddities. There also is a bookstore, ice cream parlor, and delicatessen. If you can't find what you want here, it probably doesn't exist. The Warehouse Cafe is open every day from 9 A.M. to 10 P.M. (brunch on Sundays from 9 to 2), and serves reasonably priced food amidst some of the strangest yet most pleasing decor you have ever seen: chandeliers, mirrors, lovely sideboards, secluded tables tucked away behind screens and huge pillars.

The building was indeed a warehouse during Port Costa's heyday in the 1880s and 1890s. It was built in 1886, the first fireproof building in Contra Costa County, and was used for the storage of wheat, hay, and potatoes. From the wharves, grain was loaded onto oceangoing vessels for direct shipment to Europe. Port Costa shipped more grain than San Francisco, Oakland, or Vallejo. There was also a railroad ferry across Carquinez Strait between Port Costa and Benicia; Port Costa was where the Southern Pacific landed its trains from the East en route to San Francisco.

On the corner opposite the Warehouse is the Burlington Hotel, which has been restored to offer a "turn of the century atmosphere." There are nineteen rooms, a few with private bath—but for most rooms the bath is down the hall. None of the rooms has television, radio, or telephone. No two rooms are the same, but all of them are furnished with period pieces.

This is the view down the main street of Port Costa looking toward Carquinez Strait and Benicia.

They are named for women rather than numbered, and the "atmosphere" of some is unusual if not exotic. One of them, for instance, has a beaded curtain separating sitting room from bedroom, and a round bed. The rates are reasonable; there is a Sunday through Thursday special that includes a room and two meals at the Warehouse Cafe. (Inquire at the cafe, or phone (415) 787-9973 or 787-1827.)

Next to the hotel is the Bull Valley Inn, the gourmet dining spot of Port Costa. It serves dinners in the $6-10 range. Lunch and dinner, Wednesday through Saturday, 11:30 to 9:30, and to 10:30 on Saturday. Brunch and dinner on Sunday. Closed Monday and Tuesday. (Phone 787-2244 for reservations.)

A mile and a half farther along the strait is Crockett, named for a former California Supreme Court Justice. A foundry was built here in 1882, a brick building three hundred feet long and one hundred feet wide, for the manufacture of steam threshing engines, grape-crushing equipment, and other agricultural machinery. In 1884 the largest, to that time, flour mill on the Pacific Coast was built. This mill was superseded in 1898 by a beet sugar refinery, which in 1906 became the nucleus of the California and Hawaiian Sugar Company—which now dominates Crockett's waterfront.

As you enter town, angle right on Winslow Street at the forks of the road, turn right on Vallejo Street at a "yield" sign, and continue along the waterfront on Loring Avenue. Turn left on Rolph Avenue—at the railroad station—and go to Pomona Street, the main road through town. Diagonally across the large parking lot at the corner of Loring and Rolph is "The Old Homestead," the first American home in Crockett, built in 1867 by Thomas Edwards. Edwards laid out the town in 1881 and probably gave it its name. Some of the timbers used in constructing the house were brought around the Horn. The house isn't open to the public, but you can walk around the outside.

The business district is two blocks to the right on Pomona Street. Crockett is an old town that has been spared the growth of fast-food outlets and the other roadside commercial clutter of recent years. The few neon signs in town are small and subdued, seemingly left over from thirty and forty years ago. Just walking past the stores is enough to induce instant nostalgia, though if you should wander into an antique shop you will find that a small-town storefront can conceal big-city prices.

As you leave Crockett (headed west on Pomona Street) you go under the approach to the Carquinez Bridge where you will find access to Interstate 80 going north or south. But if you want to prolong this trip a bit, and don't mind driving through countryside that soon becomes more industrial than rural, then go straight at the stop sign toward Rodeo on San Pablo Avenue. This is old U.S. 40, the main highway before the freeway was built. The road passes through a short stretch of open country—with better views of the bay than you get from the freeway—then past the Union Oil Company refinery and on to Rodeo and Pinole.

Pinole is a Mexican word—derived from Aztec—meaning meal made of ground grain or seeds. A classic early example of how San Francisco Bay has been affected by commercial civilization was provided by the experience of grain-shippers at Pinole in the nineteenth century. The first wharves were built here in 1856. They were twenty to thirty feet long, and the water at their ends was eight feet deep. As siltation reduced the depth, the wharves were lengthened. By 1882 one wharf was 2,300 feet out into the bay—and the water was still only eight feet deep at the end.

To get away from the industrial atmosphere and return to rural tranquillity, go south (left) from Pinole on Pinole Valley Road, under the freeway (I. 80), and in a couple of miles you'll be in the country. At a junction you can go left on Alhambra Valley Road to Bear Valley Road and Briones Regional Park (see *Briones and the Muir House* trip), or right on Castro Ranch Road to heavily traveled San Pablo Dam Road, and left in the direction of Orinda and access to Freeway 24. (For the map for this trip, see p. 81.)

North of Suisun Bay

Halfway between Fairfield and Rio Vista on State Route 12, in gently rolling grassland, you go over a rise and abruptly come upon an incongruous scene: fifty old railroad, interurban, and cable cars—steam, electric, and diesel—lined up on the tracks of the Sacramento Northern Railroad, and in an open-ended car barn, at Rio Vista Junction. There are ancient cable cars from early San Francisco days, San Francisco streetcars twenty-five to fifty years old, cars from the "Key Route" that crossed on the lower deck of the Bay Bridge, old Pullman cars, a parlor car—and much more.

The museum is open only on Saturdays, Sundays, and holidays from 10 A.M. to 5 P.M., and is a fascinating place for people of all ages. Much of the equipment is in working condition, and you may take a short ride on a clanging trolley or in a railroad car pulled by a steam locomotive. The museum is a project of the Bay Area Electric Railroad Association, a non-profit organization, and is a labor of love. The kids will be thrilled and adults will be nostalgic. There are fixed exhibits as well as the chance for a ride, a good-sized picnic area, and a book store selling an extensive collection of railroading books and magazines.

But half the fun is getting there, and if you don't care for railroad artifacts—or come this way on a weekday when the museum is closed—your trip should be none the less enjoyable. If you are headed east on I. 80 or north on I. 680 from the Benicia-Martinez Bridge, take the Cordelia-Green Valley Road exit, which is near the junction of the two freeways.

You will have to be alert, as there are entrances and exits and route separations and changes of direction, and it is easy to go astray. Keep in mind that you want to get off whichever freeway you're on and find your way to Cordelia, which is south and east of both freeways.

Just half a mile from the many ribbons of concrete, Cordelia has been unmarred by the headlong "progress" of the last thirty or forty years. (It was once on the main road, but was bypassed in 1929.) Though you can see the freeways perfectly well, you feel that you are traveling through a lightly-inhabited rural society. Robert H. Waterman, a clipper ship captain, settled here in 1853 and named the place Bridgeport after the city in Connecticut. When a post office was established in 1869, the Post Office Department wanted a less common name—so Waterman named it Cordelia after his wife. It is the second oldest town in Solano County (Benicia is the oldest).

If thirst is your problem, you might have a cold beer in the bar at Thompson's Corner in Cordelia—reported to be one of the oldest bars in the county—then head east on Cordelia Road toward Suisun City and Fairfield. In Suisun City turn left at the stop sign onto Main Street, and on the outskirts of Fairfield turn right where a sign points to Rio Vista—and you'll be on State Route 12.

The first excursion off of route 12 is the Grizzly Island Road, to the right just two miles east of Fairfield. After five or six miles on this road you can go to the right on a gravel road and cross a graceful, arching trestle bridge over a slough to Joice Island and the Suisun Waterfowl Refuge. If you continue on the Grizzly Island Road you will soon cross Montezuma Slough—which creates Grizzly Island—and in about three more miles come to the Fish and Wildlife Service's headquarters. You can go several miles beyond this, but eventually the road deadends and you will have to return the way you came. There are innumerable places to pull off the road and sit beside the water for a picnic lunch—or to fish, or birdwatch, or put a hat over your face and go to sleep.

After you return to route 12, head east again toward Rio Vista. If you are not going to the Railway Museum, turn right on Shiloh Road—about seven miles from Grizzly Island Road. (If you do go to the museum you can later return to Shiloh Road, or continue toward Rio Vista another one and a half miles and turn right on Collinsville Road. The latter is dirt, and not good in wet weather.) Seven miles down Shiloh Road is the crossroads hamlet of Birds Landing, named for John Bird, a native of New York, who had a storage and commission business here in the 1860s and 1870s. You may refresh yourself at the corner tavern, but even if you don't desire a libation

North of Suisun Bay

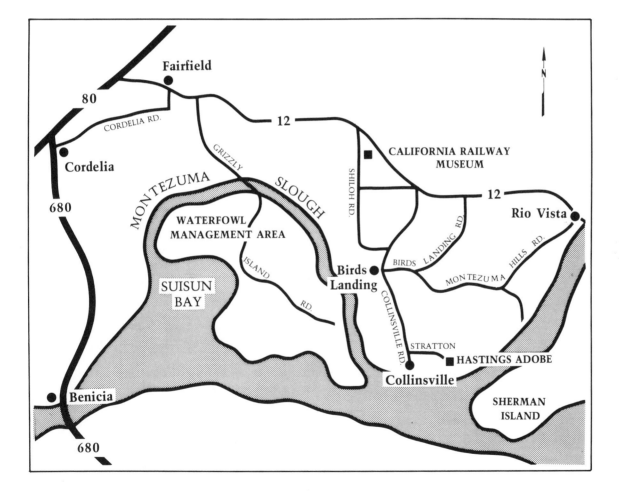

you should step inside and look at the photos on the walls—pictures from a time when Birds Landing was a more robust community than it is now.

Diagonally across the intersection is Benjamin's Store, a building erected in 1875. Mrs. Evelyn Benjamin and her husband bought the store in 1923, and Mrs. Benjamin is still there—keeping it open every day except Sunday. She was born in Birds Landing and has lived there all her life. Her mother also was born there, and her grandparents were among the area's first settlers. Anyone with an interest in local history will find Mrs. Benjamin a fine source of information, and her store a good place to pick up snacks and cold drinks.

Go on south to where the road deadends at Collinsville, on the Sacramento River. The town is merely a few houses, and was named for an early settler. It too had a time of greater economic activity, but now sports only a large fishing resort.

The last road to the left before the deadend is Stratton Lane. Go down this gravel road about one and a half miles, keeping straight ahead when the Collinsville Fishing Resort is to the right. Shortly after, the road ends at a couple of ramshackle barns and a clapboard house with the windows boarded up and a chain link fence around it. The house doesn't look like anything special, but under the clapboard is the "Montezuma Adobe," built in 1846 by Lansford W. Hastings.

Hastings twice led emigrant parties to California—in 1843 and 1845—and published *The Emigrant's Guide*, notorious for its unfounded optimism and misinformation. In the summer of 1846 Hastings went east as far as Fort Bridger (in what is now Wyoming) on the California Trail, to persuade emigrants to take his short cut, the Hastings Cutoff, south of Great Salt Lake. He managed to entice several parties—about eighty wagons in all—to follow his route, which turned out to be harder traveling and 125 miles *longer* than the existing route. The last group that year to take the Hastings Cutoff was the Donner Party. They were already traveling too late in the season for safety, but lost even more precious time following Hastings' dubious route. The Donner Party disaster, with forty people dead in the snows of the Sierra Nevada, was blamed directly on Hastings by the emigrants of 1846.

Hastings, acting as agent for the Mormons, attempted to create Montezuma City in 1847, but the so-called city never came into existence—

except for Hastings' own adobe, which is now owned by the Pacific Gas and Electric Company. The name Montezuma may seem an odd one to find in this part of the country, but it was once suggested as a new name for Alta California, and became a popular place name in the United States after the Mexican War.

Return to Birds Landing and turn right. In a mile and a half go right again on Montezuma Hills Road, a slow, winding route across the hills to Rio Vista.

The Delta

The land in the Sacramento River delta was first settled in the 1850s, but only by a transient population: men who had hoped to strike it rich in the gold fields, didn't make it, and squatted here amid a different sort of richness to raise their own food. The first levees were built in the 1870s by Chinese laborers whose herculean efforts had helped construct the Central Pacific Railroad from Sacramento to Promontory, Utah. They used shovels, wheelbarrows, and muscle power.

Now there is a complex system of canals, meandering sloughs (pronounced 'slews'), and levees to keep the water off the land. Roads wind around the perimeters of islands, often atop levees, crossing sloughs on drawbridges and quaint ferries, taking the casual motorist through a lush farmland reclaimed from tule marshes in much the way that parts of the Netherlands were reclaimed from the sea.

There is an alternate route to Interstate 80 from the Bay Area to Sacramento through the heart of the delta. You can take State Route 4 past Antioch to State Route 160, cross the Antioch bridge, and follow along the many bends of the Sacramento River. This can be used simply as a route to Sacramento, with stops at interesting places along the way; or you can devise one or more loop trips on either side of the river. You can even make it an all-day excursion, going up the river one way and coming back down another. We have written it as an all-day tour.

The first opportunity to get off route 160 comes just a mile past the end

of the Antioch bridge. Turn right on the Sherman Island Levee Road which takes you due south through low-lying farmland before climbing onto the levee along the San Joaquin River. Levee roads are invariably narrow and have steep banks. A large sign cautions against parking on the road, but there are innumerable wide spots where you can pull off to fish or picnic. The need for the levee is obvious: the land is plainly below the river level. The island is named for Sherman Day, who owned a ranch here and was a one-term State Senator in the 1850s and U.S. Surveyor General for California from 1868 to 1871. And therein lies a lesson on how to have a place named for yourself: come early, own land, and get elected to public office.

Halfway up the island you'll find a place to get gas, ice, bait, and rent a houseboat. At the north end is a larger, more modern establishment that also rents houseboats and serves food and drink. Eventually the levee road returns you to route 160. Turn right across the bridge, and in a short distance is the entrance to Brannan Island State Recreation Area, where there are picnic tables. (The day use fee is $1.50.) This island is named for Samuel Brannan, known for his entrepreneurial activities in various places in central California. He came to California in 1846 as the organizer of Mormon colonization, made his first big money from gold mining, and became wealthy in real estate and other financial ventures. He was one of the founders of Yuba City, and was the founder, promoter, and builder of the first health spa at Calistoga—which he also named. Yet despite all this, Brannan Island is the only place that bears his name.

A mile and a quarter beyond the park entrance turn right on Twitchell Island Road. When you come to a fork in the road take either branch—they run along opposite sides of Sevenmile Slough and come together several miles farther on. From that point you can continue along the slough on Brannan Island Road until it brings you to State Route 12, or you can turn left on Jackson Slough Road and go four miles to Isleton on the Sacramento River.

Isleton, "The Asparagus Center of the World," is the heart of an area that produces about half of the U.S. asparagus crop, and 90 percent of the world's supply of canned asparagus. Route 160, with modern cafes and service stations, runs along the edge of Isleton, but the interesting part of town is the photogenic old main street. Park your car and walk around. There are several markets, cafes, and other businesses, but half the buildings are deserted and the town looks as though time has stood still for it for

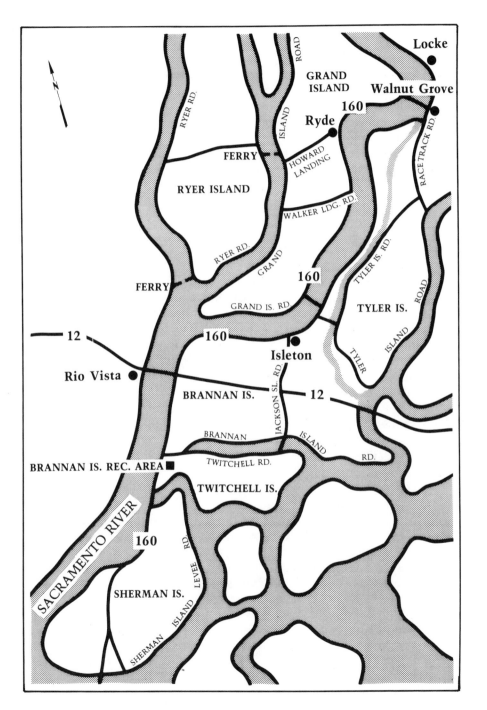

Lower Delta

99

the past forty years. Many of the inhabitants are elderly Chinese, and this unique town, though still standing, seems to be dying—gradually on its way to becoming a ghost town.

Half a mile upriver from Isleton on 160, turn right on the Tyler Island Bridge Road, and turn right again after crossing the bridge. You will cross the lower end of the island, then go up onto a levee—this one along the North Fork of the Mokelumne River. It's as slow and leisurely a drive as can be imagined—almost entirely without traffic. At the north end of the island bear to the right on Race Track Road and go to Walnut Grove. Just outside of town, at the junction of county route J-11, a turn to the right takes you—in half a mile—to Giusti's Restaurant. This is an Italian family-style place that has a reputation for good food and modest prices. It serves lunch and dinner, and is closed Mondays.

From below Isleton to Freeport—eight miles from Sacramento—there are roads on both sides of the river. Route 160 begins on the east side, crosses to the west above Isleton, and then back to the east below Court-land. The road across from 160 invariably has less traffic.

Walnut Grove is another town for parking and walking. The river road is on a level with the second stories of buildings in the town. The old, ramshackle, and partly deserted Chinese section may not last many more years. The extremely weathered wood of the buildings looks as though it's ready to turn to dust at a touch. On up the road a mile is Locke, another old Chinese town. Park off the highway and take a stroll along the main street, which is so narrow that two vehicles constitute a traffic jam. Although Locke looks to be at least a century old, it was actually built in 1916 after a fire destroyed most of the Chinatown of Walnut Grove.

As you go on upriver you pass through extensive pear orchards. The heavy traffic of route 160 crosses to the east side at Courtland, once mostly a Chinese town but now largely Chicano. Farther along is Hood, and a short side trip is in order for those with an interest in historical footnotes. There is a cemetery at Franklin, a crossroads four miles east of Hood. Here is the grave (a State Historical Landmark) of Alexander Hamilton Willard, one of the last survivors of the Lewis and Clark Expedition. He was born in New Hampshire in 1777, but did not come to California until 1852—and died in 1865.

Freeport was indeed true to its name when it was established in 1862 as a shipping center in competition with Sacramento, which taxed goods

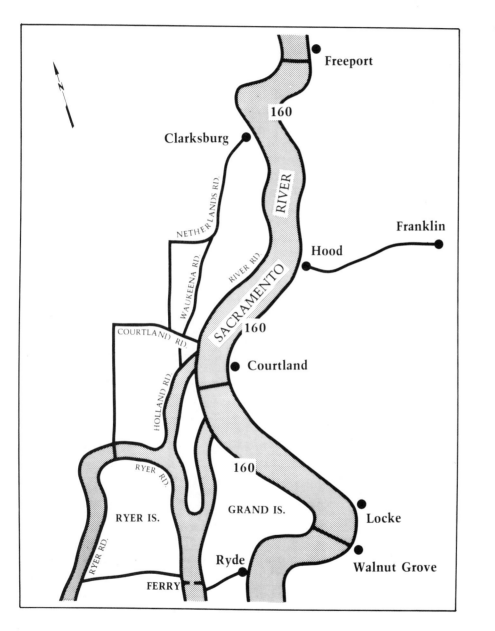

crossing the levee. In the center of town on the right is A. J. Bump's, built in 1863 as a general store and saloon. It has been restored, serves food and strong drink, and is worth entering to look at the artifacts and old photos. Two miles on up the road is the present end—or beginning—of Interstate 5, which will reconnect you with the Big World. Following route 160 will take you into downtown Sacramento.

If you are returning to the Bay Area, a different route with different experiences awaits your pleasure. Cross to the west side of the river on the bridge just below Freeport, and go downriver four miles to Clarksburg. Turn right on Netherlands Road—the second road in the center of town—and go five miles to Waukeena Road, a left turn. Waukeena Road soon gets onto the levee along Elk Slough, which is a slow drive for about seven miles to the southern end of this particular island. Toward the end the name changes to Holland Road, but simply keep straight on along the slough.

At the road's end turn left across the bridge to Ryer Island. In the 1850s the entire island was owned by W. M. Ryer, a Stockton physician, who once made a large contribution to public health by vaccinating some 2,000 San Joaquin Valley Indians.

Aside from the bridge that you have just crossed, Ryer Island is connected to other parts of the delta by two ferries. These are free—operated by Caltrans—and are open twenty-four hours. (Other ferries in the delta are county-operated.) There is a road entirely around the periphery of Ryer Island, and an east-west road straight across the middle—take whichever you wish. Our suggestion is that you turn left after crossing the bridge and continue until you reach Howard Landing Ferry and cross over on the good ship *J. Mack*, which operates on a cable. Go to the right when you reach the other side, and then left in half a mile at Howard Landing. Three miles across the fields of Grand Island brings you to Ryde on the Sacramento River. The name comes from a town on the Isle of Wight in the English Channel. Its notable feature is the Ryde Hotel, built in the mid-1920s. It's a favorite watering place for those driving from the Bay Area to Sacramento, but even if you don't want to eat, drink, or sleep, stop in anyway to sample the atmosphere. (It will probably be closed during the first three months of the year.) If you should want to throw a banquet in a unique spot, this is it. (Telephone: (916) 776-1481.)

Go downriver from Ryde one and a half miles, turn right on Walker Landing Road, and go back across Grand Island. During times of heavy rains some of this land is under water. If you want to take more time and drive along the rivers and sloughs, keep headed south on route 160. Where 160 turns left across the river, keep straight on and make a loop around the southern end of Grand Island. Either of these routes gets you to Walker Landing and Howard Landing. Just south of Walker Landing, along Steamboat Slough, is the Hogback Island Recreation Facility, with an attractive shaded picnic ground.

Return to the Howard Landing Ferry and take another cruise back to Ryer Island on the *J. Mack*. Make your way to the south end of the island by either route, following the signs to Rio Vista. You cross to the mainland on the Ryer Island Ferry, on a vessel named *The Real McCoy* because it is the delta's only free-running ferry: it isn't hooked to a cable, and arrives at the other side due to the skill of the skipper.

There is one other stop to be made before you conclude your tour. A mile or so down the road to Rio Vista from the ferry is an unused shipyard. It's locked and guarded, so you can't get in, but its most noted occupant is in plain view: the *Delta King*, once a luxurious sternwheeler that—with its sister ship the *Delta Queen*—made nightly trips between San Francisco and Sacramento. The Delta King's hull was built in Glasgow, Scotland, and shipped, in pieces, to Stockton in 1927 where it was assembled and lavishly furnished. During the 1930s it carried as many as 1,000 passengers on a trip taking just over ten hours. The highest priced accommodation was a stateroom on the upper deck for five dollars, which included your meals. The Second World War brought an end to the river cruises, and after performing various sorts of utilitarian work both ships were put into the mothball fleet in Carquinez Strait at the end of the war. The *Delta Queen* was sold to the Green Lines of Cincinnati, was completely restored, and still makes trips on the Ohio and Mississippi Rivers. In February, 1978, the *Delta King* was sold at auction. Its new owner plans to have it towed to San Francisco and converted into a floating dockside restaurant.

At Rio Vista is the junction with State Route 12 and—across the bridge —State Route 160, the way back to the Bay Area. To get onto the bridge, turn left through an underpass and take the looping on-ramp to the right.

East of Mt. Diablo

William H. Brewer, in October, 1861, visited the Black Diamond coal mines northeast of Mt. Diablo:

> . . . in this great mass is a bed of coal over four feet thick. The bed, like the strata in which it is found, is inclined about forty-five degrees. Several mines are opened, and companies have formed with capital to the amount of some three or four million dollars. They are now getting perhaps a hundred tons per day and making preparations for more extensive work.

The mines were indeed expanded. Several towns sprang up—settled by Welsh and English coal miners—and three railroads were built from the mines to wharves on the Sacramento River. But the coal was low grade, the capital investment high, and a mine explosion in 1876 marked the beginning of a long decline in activity until all mining stopped in 1902.

The East Bay Regional Park District has opened the area to daytime hiking and picnicking. To reach the mines, take the Somersville Road exit from route 4 at Antioch and go south toward the hills. The road leads up a shallow valley. At places you can see, on the left, the grade of the former Pittsburg Railroad—and even one of the old brick culverts. At the end of the road are some cattle pens and a few picnic tables, but no water. The former road can be followed on foot, and in a fourth of a mile you come to the site of Somersville, named after Francis Somers, one of the men who discovered the coal vein in 1859. Here is a water tap, and a dozen picnic tables shaded by oak and buckeye trees.

This is the beginning of an extensive network of trails of varying lengths and degrees of difficulty—enough variety to satisfy everyone from the ardent hiker to those who would rather husband their energies for the week ahead. Hikers should always carry water, as any water found while on the trail is not considered fit to drink.

From 1922 to 1949 there was renewed mining activity in the Black Diamond area for the production of silica sand. At the site of Somersville is the entrance to one of these sand-mining tunnels. Heavy iron gates bar the entrance, but you can see into the tunnel for a considerable distance. The timbering is in remarkably good condition, and even on the hottest day a refreshing cool breeze will be blowing out through the gates. The Park District operates weekend guided tours through this mine, including a visit to Greathouse Portal, a huge underground room. The tours are limited to twenty people, so you must make reservations in advance. (Telephone (415) 757-2620 for times and reservations.)

An interesting and not difficult hike is to the Rose Hill Cemetery that served Somersville and Nortonville. The latter town was named for Noah Norton, a native of New York, who located the Black Diamond Mine and built the first house in town. As you walk up the road from the parking lot toward Somersville, look uphill to your right and you will see five Italian cypresses marking the location of the cemetery. You reach the cemetery by continuing up the road from the Somersville picnic area. Many of the headstones have been knocked down by vandals, but they are otherwise in good shape and the inscriptions are quite legible. *Gone by sight but not by memory.*

Although no buildings remain at the townsites, and it may be hard to imagine two towns with a combined population of nearly 1,000 in places now marked only by mine tailings, Nortonville and Somersville were—in their time—the largest cities in Contra Costa County.

A roundabout route to the Black Diamond Preserve—one requiring slow driving over winding roads—is by way of Clayton. Take Clayton Road from Concord—or Ygnacio Valley Road from Walnut Creek to Clayton Road where you turn right—and go through Clayton. Just at the edge of town where the main road bends right, go straight ahead across a bridge and you're on Black Diamond Way. A sign reads *Impassable in Wet Weather*, and it should be believed. The road starts with a gravel surface but soon becomes dirt—sometimes a bit rough in places but easy to drive in any sort of vehicle—and winds uphill beside an oak-lined stream bed. It's about four miles to the crest, from where you have a fine view down

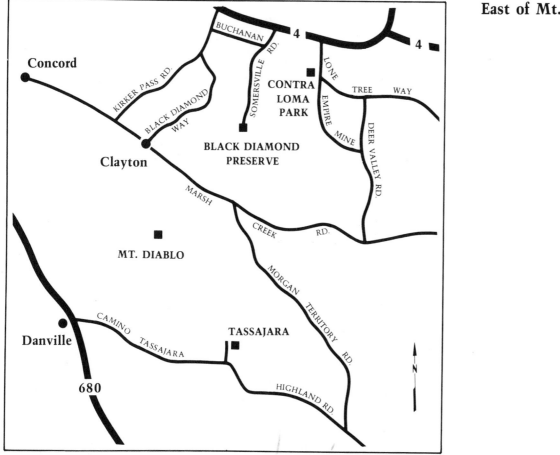

East of Mt. Diablo

toward Antioch and across the Sacramento River. The road is paved from the crest down the other side, though it is steep, winding, and about one and a half lanes wide. Halfway down the hill it becomes Nortonville Road, which you follow to Kirker Pass Road, turn right to Buchanan Road (the first traffic light), go three miles to Somersville Road, and right again.

There is a long way around to get back to wherever you started. Take the Lone Tree Way exit south from route 4 (one mile east of the Somersville Road exit.) Where Lone Tree Way turns left at the Antioch airport (three and a half miles), continue straight south on Empire Mine Road. You will pass the entrance to Contra Loma Regional Park (picnicking and swimming; open 7 A.M. to 8 P.M.; parking $2.00 per vehicle on weekends and holidays, $1.00 on weekdays), and leave most of the traffic behind. The road crosses several low ridges and serene valleys, with an ever-changing view of the east side of Mt. Diablo, and no sign of economic activity other than an occasional cattle ranch. Go right on Deer Valley Road, and right again on Marsh Creek Road, which takes you back to Clayton.

Should you have the time to extend your jaunt and enjoy a slow drive over one of the more remote roads in Contra Costa County, turn sharp left on Morgan Territory Road about five miles before Clayton. In a mile you are past the houses and winding through dense woods along Marsh Creek. In six or seven miles you cross a watershed, the trees abruptly disappear, and there is a wide view to the south and east across the rolling hills. The road winds down to Highland Road, where you turn right and go about six miles to Camino Tassajara (Spanish for a place where jerked beef is hung to dry). Left at this junction takes you to I. 580 to go east toward Stockton or west toward Oakland. But go right for two miles, and where Camino Tassajara bends to the left, keep straight ahead on Finley Road. A mile up this road is a well-preserved, photogenic, nineteenth-century schoolhouse. Northwest of the intersection of Finley Road and Camino Tassajara was the location of Tassajara—nothing remains to be seen. Bret Harte visited Tassajara in the fall of 1856 while a camp meeting was going on. He used the locale and a description of the meeting in his story, "An Apostle of the Tules." Harte was excessively harsh on the landscape, saying that a more "barren, dreary, monotonous, and uninviting landscape never stretched before human eye." He was also harsh on some of the denizens, referring to the boys and young men on the outskirts of the meeting as being "acrimonious with disappointed curiosity, lazy without the careless ease of vagrancy, and vicious without the excitement of dissipation." There are many opportunities for dissipation these days—you will not encounter the descendants of Harte's characters, and the landscape is actually quite lovely.

Continue westward on Camino Tassajara which takes you to Danville and I. 680, which runs north toward Walnut Creek. Though it may seem anticlimactic to join the throng on the freeway, you have escaped for a day to the site of a town that has risen and fallen and left hardly a trace, and on your return driven through a landscape scarcely changed in historic times.

Byron-Brentwood-
John Marsh House

Someday when you are returning to the Bay Area from Los Angeles or the Sierra, end your trip with a slow, relaxed tour through Byron, Brentwood, and the tranquil fruit and nut orchards of eastern Contra Costa County.

If you are westbound on Interstate 205, take the Grant Line Road exit, go west one mile to Byron Road (county route J-4), and turn right toward Antioch. If you are headed north on I. 580, take the Patterson Pass Road exit and go north about four miles to Byron Road, then left.

Five miles north of the county line is the town of Byron. The photogenic old main street is a block to the left of the highway. More than half the buildings are empty, and the overall appearance is that of an abandoned movie set. The dominant—and obviously most prosperous—establishment is the Wild Idol Inn. (If you want to know where the name comes from you will have to go in and ask.) There is also a market, and an antique shop open only from 1:30 to 5:30 on Thursday, Friday, and Saturday. Forty years ago Byron had a population of 400, but its fortunes seem to have declined since then.

Not far from town is Byron Hot Springs, once a flourishing resort. In 1882 there were five cottages, and a hotel with accommodations for forty guests. The hotel burned in 1912, but it was rebuilt and the resort operated until the Second World War. There were three types of springs, each reputed to be beneficial in a different way or for different ailments: a salt spring at 122°F, a white sulphur spring at 70°F, and a Liver and Kidney spring at 58°F.

The war brought a peculiar interlude in the life of Byron Hot Springs. In 1942, the War Department took over, renamed it Camp Tracy, and spent $10,000 converting it into a center for interrogating prisoners of war. The army remodeled the hotel, pump house, fire house, and eleven cabins. During 1944 more than nine hundred Japanese and six hundred German prisoners were interrogated, although the maximum number there at any one time was about fifty. The army closed down its operation on September 1, 1945, and the place reverted to a hot springs. Unfortunately, "taking the waters" had fallen out of favor, and whatever remains of the Byron Hot Springs resort is now private property and cannot be entered.

Go west from Byron on Camino Diablo Road about five miles to the junction of Marsh Creek Road, which turns off to the right. In a bit over a mile stop at the high point of this road—just above the Marsh Creek Reservoir—read the historical marker on the right, then drive a few hundred feet farther for an incongruous sight on your left. A tenth of a mile from the road is a three-story stone house looking like an aged import from England. The house is more than 120 years old. It was built in 1856 by John Marsh, the first American settler in what is now Contra Costa County. "Doctor" Marsh came to this region in 1837 and bought the Rancho los Medanos (sand hills or dunes). He had a Bachelor of Arts degree from Harvard, which the Mexican authorities—because they couldn't read Latin—accepted as a medical degree, and Marsh was given a license to practice medicine. He preferred to be paid in cattle for his services, and by the early 1850s had a herd of several thousand head. Marsh was kind and generous to the Indians, but suspicious and tight-fisted in his dealings with Mexicans and American settlers. When the Bartleson-Bidwell party, the first group of emigrants to cross the Sierra, arrived at Marsh's rancho in 1841, minus their wagons and most of their belongings, Marsh welcomed them hospitably—and then demanded a stiff payment for his generosity.

Marsh lived in an adobe house for more than fifteen years, but after he married in 1851 he determined to build a fine permanent house for his bride—a blend of manor house and castle. His wife died before the house was finished, and just a few weeks after it was completed Marsh himself was murdered on the road by three Mexicans.

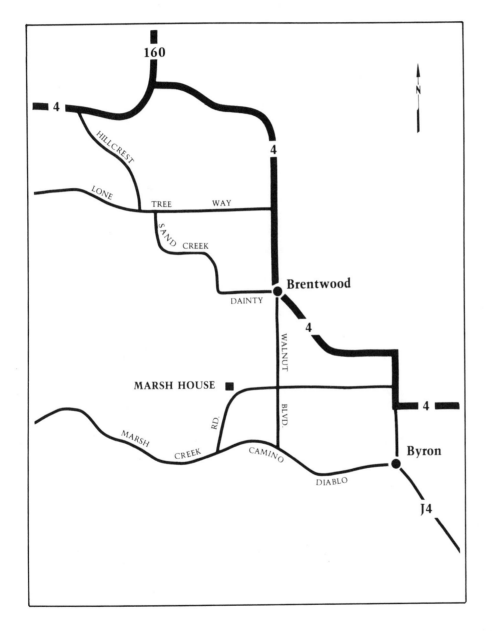

Byron—Brentwood

The fourteen-room house is built of cream-colored freestone from a nearby quarry. It has arched windows, peaked roofs and gables, projecting eaves, and a central tower sixty-five feet high. Gabled windows in the attic look east, west, and south. There is a ten-foot-wide piazza around three sides of the house, supported by octagonal pillars, and over this is a walk enclosed by a balustrade. The original top of the tower was crenelated. It was knocked off by an earthquake in 1868, and replaced with the present wooden top of a plain style.

After Marsh's death his estate was involved in lengthy litigation, and it was a number of years before it came into the hands of his son and daughter. When William H. Brewer passed by the house in June of 1862, he described its occupant as "a boor," and the house and grounds in a sorry state: ". . . old chairs with rawhide bottoms occupy rooms with marble mantels . . . with hogs in the yard, some of the windows broken, and things slovenly in general."

Though the house and seven acres around it are owned by the county, this tract is surrounded by private property—and the public has no access. The house has been uninhabited since the 1920s, and has suffered considerable deterioration. However, the house and its surrounding land have been added to the State Park System. The house will be restored, an Indian artifact museum will be built, and in time they will be opened to the public.

Continue on Marsh Creek Road to Walnut Boulevard, then turn left and go to Brentwood—about four miles. The name comes from a village in Essex, England, the ancestral home of John Marsh. There is a well-shaded park in the center of town—a good spot for a picnic. Across the street from the park is the city hall, where you can acquire a copy of "Harvest Time," a list, including a map, of more than twenty farms in the vicinity where you can buy produce directly from the farmer. In some cases you can pick the fruits and vegetables yourself. You can also get a copy by sending a stamped, self-addressed envelope to: Harvest Time, P.O. Box O, Brentwood, CA 94513. Within two miles of the Marsh house, for example, there are four farms where, in season, you can pick cherries, apricots, boysenberries, nectarines, and peaches.

If you are not in a rush and still would like to follow the country roads, go west out of Brentwood on Dainty Avenue. Turn right on Fairview

Avenue, left on Sand Creek Road, and left again on Long Tree Way, which is the only road on this route with an appreciable amount of traffic. You follow it for three-tenths of a mile before you turn right on Hillcrest Road, which takes you to the freeway, State Route 4.

The roads from Brentwood to route 4 are through fruit and nut orchards. Occasionally you pass the property of someone who has crops both above and below the ground: oil wells amid the orchards. To the city dweller, it looks like the best of all possible worlds.

Altamont Pass-
Patterson Pass-Corral Hollow

The next time you travel Interstate 580 going to or from the Sierra, the San Joaquin Valley, or Los Angeles, take the time to explore one of the alternate roads across the hills of the Livermore Range. There are three possibilities, any one of which can be used for a one-way trip or can be combined with one of the others to make a loop.

North of 580 is the Altamont Pass Road, which until 1938 was the main highway, old U.S. 50. But long before it became part of the state and federal highway systems, the Altamont Pass route was well known and heavily traveled. In 1849 a large tent was erected at Mountain House east of the range, and an enterprising man kept a "house of entertainment" and sold "refreshments" to miners on their way to the gold fields. The Oakland-Stockton stage changed horses at Mountain House, and the locale developed into a camp for stockmen, rancheros, and immigrants. The Central Pacific Railroad (now the Southern Pacific) laid its tracks through the pass in 1869, and gave the name Altamont to the highest spot of what was then called Livermore Pass.

Going east on 580, take the Greenville-Altamont Pass Road exit, go under the freeway, and turn right on the old road that follows up the valley with the Southern Pacific and Western Pacific tracks. There is little traffic now on this former main highway; on weekdays, perhaps only twenty or thirty vehicles an hour. Though not far from the freeway it has the appearance and feel of isolated country, and if you're lucky you may see a golden eagle flying low across the valley. In 1898 there were a dozen houses, a hotel, post office, school, and a railroad depot at Altamont. In 1940 Altamont had a population of sixty-eight, which, by all appearances, has dwindled to a handful.

As you near the summit—a lofty 741 feet above sea level—an old service station and garage is on the right. An indication of how long it has been since this was a going business are the two gasoline pumps: they're of the old gravity flow type. You hand-pumped the required amount of gas into the glass top, stuck the nozzle into the car's filler spout, and gravity did the rest. You never had to worry about power failures.

A short distance past the garage is a long-abandoned schoolhouse, and then there's an overpass across the tracks and you're on the downgrade toward Mountain House and the San Joaquin Valley. It is difficult today to imagine what this curving two-lane road was like before the new road was built. Trucks were relatively under-powered in those days, and crawled up the grades with long strings of exasperated motorists behind them.

Mountain House is six miles east of the pass. An adobe house replaced the tent in about 1860, and a frame building was later added to the adobe. Eventually these were torn down, and a permanent residence built on the site. That too is gone, and now there are a few dwellings and a quaint old Shell station and a tavern. From here you can return to the freeway at an interchange one mile west, go south to the Altamont Speedway and Patterson Pass Road, or north four miles on Mountain House Road to the junction of Byron Road—county route J-4. To get on Altamont Pass Road westbound, take the Grant Line Rd.-Byron exit from I. 580 just west of the junction of 580 and 205. Turn right at the foot of the off-ramp, go four tenths of a mile to Altamont Pass Road, and turn left.

The second alternate to the Freeway is Patterson Pass Road. Headed east on 580, take the Greenville-Altamont Pass Road exit and go south on Greenville Road about a mile and a half to Patterson Pass Road. It's a narrow and steep road, especially on the east side, and is less-traveled than Altamont Pass. It will take twice as long to drive as the Altamont Pass route, and will reward you with a spectacular view of the San Joaquin Valley as you plunge down from the high point. On a clear day you can see the Sierra with ease.

Altamont and Patterson Passes

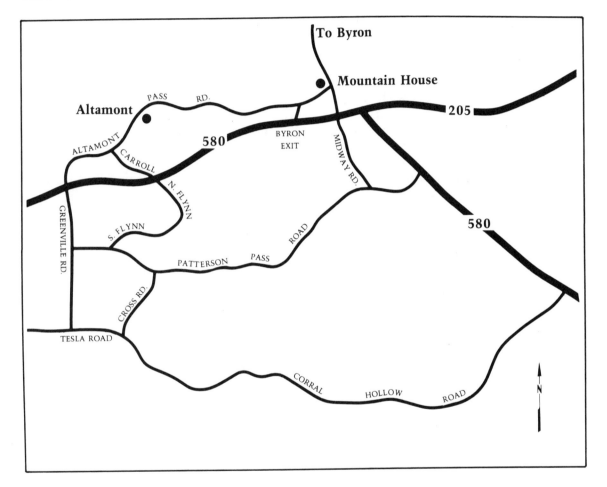

The story has it that Patterson Pass was named for the wife of Andrew Jackson Patterson, who settled in the area in the 1850s. One day while driving through the pass, the Pattersons' wagon was overturned by a strong wind, and Mrs. Patterson suffered a broken leg—and the name of Patterson stuck to the pass. There must be easier ways to achieve immortality.

As you come onto the plain you pass a large PG & E substation. This is at or near the site of Midway, a former stop on the Central Pacific. Midway between what two places we are not sure, but probably San Francisco and Sacramento. You can go north from here on Midway Road to Mountain House—about two and a half miles—or continue on Patterson Pass Road to an interchange at I. 580. The western ends of Altamont and Patterson Pass Roads are connected by S. Flynn, N. Flynn, and Carroll Roads. This connection crosses I. 580 at its summit—an intersection—and is an attractive drive in its own right.

The third alternate is farther south yet—the next interchange south on the freeway from Patterson Pass Road. In San Joaquin County it's called Corral Hollow Road, and in Alameda County it's Tesla Road. The name of Tesla Road—and the town of Tesla, which is long gone—come from Nicola Tesla, an Austro-American inventor of electrical devices.

Corral Hollow Road going west from I. 580 follows a wide valley for half the distance to Livermore, but where Corral Hollow Creek curves around to the southeast the road leaves the valley, climbs steeply to the top of the ridge, and goes abruptly down the other side. There is one stretch, before you can see into Livermore Valley, where you look west-southwest across several rows of hills. There is no road nor building nor any sign of human existence, and you will swear that you have come upon an uninhabited, pristine country—a glimpse of the prospect that greeted the early travelers and explorers. This route has more traffic than the other two, but not so much as to spoil the enjoyment of a leisurely drive—except perhaps on weekends.

Corral Hollow saw some minor-league coal mining in the nineteenth century. In the late 1890s, though, it seemed to those involved that they were headed for the big time. A railroad had been built from the mines to Stockton, but even grander—or grandiose—plans were in the offing. There was a scheme afoot to build an electric generating plant at the mines which would furnish power to Oakland, and to build an electric railroad to

Livermore and Oakland—but it never happened.

Before the coal mining, Corral Hollow was, for a season, the province of Grizzly Adams, who came here in 1855 because he had heard there were many mountain lions, grizzlies, and other game. This was at the time of the "Kern River excitement," and Adams and another man made a living selling venison to the hundreds of people coming through Livermore Pass and Corral Hollow on their way to the mines.

In October, 1861, William H. Brewer camped near the ruins of Adams' cabin in Corral Hollow, and talked to a man who had hunted with Adams and had remained there when Adams left. "We had a good time before the settlers came," he said, and told Brewer that he had killed 700 or 800 deer since he had come there but that they were getting scarce. Small wonder!

The story of Adams' life is a classic: much more dramatic and stirring than the trumped-up fare provided by television. Adams' experiences in Corral Hollow, the Sierra Nevada, the Rockies, and elsewhere in the West are recounted in *The Adventures of James Capen Adams, Mountaineer and Grizzly Bear Hunter of California*, by Theodore H. Hittell.

Mines Road-
Lick Observatory

This is an all-day trip through the most remote parts of Alameda and Santa Clara Counties. You go from the vineyards of Livermore Valley to an observatory atop a four-thousand-foot mountain, and back down to near sea level at San Jose.

Take the Livermore Avenue exit from I. 580 and go south straight through the center of Livermore. South of town the street name changes to Tesla Avenue. The town itself was named for Robert Livermore, an English sailor who had the good sense to jump ship—in 1822—to seek his fortune in California. He eventually owned most of what is now Livermore Valley, and became a wealthy cattle rancher and horticulturist.

Livermore is your last chance to buy provisions, as there are only two modest cafes and no stores from here to the outskirts of San Jose. Two miles south of town, on your left, is the Concannon Winery, established in 1883. (The tasting and sales room is open Monday through Saturday, 9 to 4; and on Sunday from noon to 4:30. Tours are given Monday through Friday on the hour from 9 to 3, except noon; Saturday and Sunday, on the hour from noon to 3.)

Your route goes right on Mines Road a short distance past Concannon, but you might take the time to visit Wente Brothers Winery—on Tesla Road about half a mile past Mines Road. Wente also was founded in 1883, and is one of only a few wineries in the state still owned and operated by the original families. There are tours Monday through Saturday, 9 to 5; Sunday, 11 to 3:30. Tasting on weekends only.

Return to Mines Road, and you are headed off through vineyards toward a lightly inhabited and little traveled country. At four miles bear to the left, as the road straight ahead goes only to Del Valle State Recreation Area. You wind along Arroyo Mocho for several miles past farms and ranches, but soon the arroyo becomes narrow and steep-sided, and the road climbs—with many curves—up the left side. Mocho means 'cut-off creek,' a name given because the stream has no outlet but simply spreads out into many smaller streams between Livermore and Pleasanton and sinks into the ground.

There are fine views going up this canyon, and back the way you have come. About seventeen miles from Livermore is the Branding Iron Cafe, dispensing coffee, beer, and snacks. Beyond this point the road loses its center line and narrows a bit as it winds among scattered oaks and pines. For about five miles the way is through open range—no fences—and you may find cattle disputing the right of way with the occasional vehicle. The road widens to a full two lanes at the Santa Clara County line. Eight miles farther on is the junction with Del Puerto Canyon Road where there is a Shell station and a bar that serves coffee, drinks, and snacks. Del Puerto Canyon Road goes eastward for about twenty miles to Interstate 5. This is a way to approach either the Mt. Hamilton or Arroyo Mocho to Livermore routes, or to go out to the freeway if you are headed for Los Angeles.

On San Antonio Valley Road just south of the junction is a sign suggesting that the road is not advisable for cars pulling trailers—sound advice even for those who don't believe in signs. From the junction to Mt. Hamilton is eighteen and a half miles. Four miles along, the direction changes abruptly from south to west. After climbing a bit you follow down along a creek into Isabel Valley, cross the valley, and start up the winding grade to Mt. Hamilton. When you are most of the way up, pull off the road and enjoy the great views to the north and east over country that appears untouched.

You will come upon the Lick Observatory without warning. Round a bend in the road, and there it is—looking almost too big to be real and too strange to be of human origin. There are two buildings open to the public on a daily basis—every day of the year except Thanksgiving and Christmas.

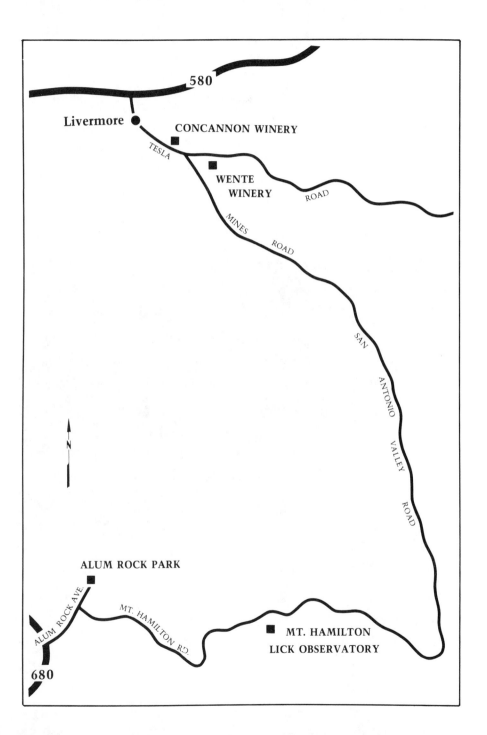

580

Livermore

CONCANNON WINERY

TESLA

WENTE
WINERY

ROAD

MINES ROAD

SAN ANTONIO VALLEY ROAD

N

ALUM ROCK PARK

ALUM ROCK AVE.

MT. HAMILTON RD.

MT. HAMILTON
LICK OBSERVATORY

680

The building that houses the 120-inch telescope dominates Lick Observatory atop Mt. Hamilton.

The first is the visitor's gallery of the 120-inch telescope. (Open 10 to 5.) On the right side of the road are a small parking area, and a sign directing you to a short uphill walk.

The second is the main building, reached by driving up a narrow road—turn left at the forks, where the right fork goes downhill toward San Jose. (The building is open 1 to 5.) An attendant shows visitors the 36-inch telescope and gives a short talk on the observatory, at fifteen minutes before and after the hour. There are many superb photographs in the main hall, a seismograph with a good explanation of how it works, and you can buy photos, postcards, and booklets.

The observatory also operates a summer visitors' program on Friday evenings from early July to mid-September, the only times the public may look through any of the telescopes. There is a lecture by one of the astronomers, and each visitor has the opportunity to look at selected astronomical objects through both the 12-inch and 36-inch telescopes. The numbers are limited at these Friday evening programs, and you must write for tickets in advance. Send a stamped, self-addressed envelope to: Summer Visitors' Program, Lick Observatory, Mt. Hamilton, CA 95140.

The first white men to climb Mt. Hamilton were William H. Brewer and Charles Hoffmann of the Whitney Survey, and Laurentine Hamilton, a Presbyterian minister—for whom the peak was named—on August 26, 1861. In 1876, James Lick, an eccentric millionaire who made his money in real estate speculation, died and left an endowment of $700,000 for the establishment of an observatory on Mt. Hamilton. The site was granted by an act of Congress, the county built a road to the summit, and the observatory was opened to the public in 1888. Lick is buried beneath a supporting pillar of one of the telescopes.

From the observatory it is nineteen miles down a crooked road to the outskirts of San Jose. If you're lucky enough to be making this trip on one of the infrequent clear days, you will see the Santa Clara Valley, the coastal hills, and the southern end of San Francisco Bay spread out below you like a gigantic relief map. If you came up this way, as most people do, by all means continue to Livermore.

The Mt. Hamilton Road meets Alum Rock Park Avenue about five miles from San Jose. To the right is Alum Rock Park (picnicking, swimming, horseback riding), and to the left two miles is the junction with Interstate 680.

The Coast
South of San Francisco

State Route 1 runs south from San Francisco, at first clinging to rugged cliffs above the surf, and later passing through farmland between the hills of the San Francisco peninsula and the dunes and wide, sandy beaches along the coast. Once you get south of Pacifica the road is two lanes, carrying a considerable burden of fast-moving traffic. There are so many state and county beaches between San Francisco and Santa Cruz that we won't attempt to list them. The beaches are where the throng goes, especially on sunny weekends, and we propose to take you on the unfrequented back roads that parallel much of the coastal highway.

You get onto route 1 either by following the route number south from the Golden Gate Bridge, or by following Interstate 280 past Daly City where route 1 cuts off and goes over to the coast near Pacifica. About two miles after the freeway ends, turn left at Linda Mar Avenue (a traffic signal), and go eight tenths of a mile to the Sanchez Adobe, which is on the right just past the third signal on Linda Mar.

The Sanchez Adobe, shaded by tall trees, is a handsome and well-preserved two-story ranch house built in 1842-46 by Francisco Sanchez. The building occupies part of the site of a former rancho, or outpost, of Mission Dolores in San Francisco. The house that preceded the Sanchez Adobe is said to have been built partly with timbers from a ship that was wrecked on nearby San Pedro Point early in the 1800s. After Sanchez died in 1862, the house passed through the hands of several owners and was put to a variety of uses: hunting lodge, saloon, packing shed for artichokes. It is owned by San Mateo County, and operated by the County Parks and Recreation Department. The hours and days it is open are somewhat uncertain at present, and it might be wise to phone the Parks and Recreation Department in Redwood City. (415–364-5600, Ext. 2486.)

The house has been nicely restored, and furnished with attractive period pieces. On the ground floor, in the dining room, are a three-corner cupboard, and two highchairs with wheels. In another room are various artifacts unearthed during excavations: tools, spikes, bottles, cutlery, and horseshoes. Upstairs is a parlor with piano and marbletop table, and there are two bedrooms, one with a cradle, a spinning wheel, and a closet full of old dresses.

Return to route 1 and continue south. As you pass across Devils Slide you are following the line of the Ocean Shore Railroad, which ran south from San Francisco from 1906 to 1920. Straight ahead of you is a V-shaped gap known as Saddle Cut, which was created by the railroad construction crews who used nine tons of black powder in a single explosion. The story of the Ocean Shore can be found in a well-written and handsomely illustrated book, *The Last Whistle*, by Jack R. Wagner.

As you go down into the rolling country south of the mountains, you are traveling, in reverse, along the route of the exploring party led by Don Gaspar de Portolá. This group, the first white men to come into California by land, left San Diego on July 14, 1769, to search for the Bay of Monterey which had been described by Vizcaíno in 1602 as being a place of unsurpassed beauty and "sheltered from all winds." Portolá reached the vicinity of Monterey in early October, actually saw the small bay at Carmel, but didn't recognize Monterey Bay—probably because it was obscured by fog. So he pushed on north, still looking for Monterey Bay—and discovered San Francisco Bay instead. The locations of many of Portolá's campsites are known with a fair degree of accuracy. On October 30, 1769, the party was camped just north of Montara Beach.

Just south of Moss Beach is the James V. Fitzgerald Marine Reserve. Keep an eye peeled for the sign on the right, and go down that side street for several blocks. This has long been a popular place for collecting mollusks and other creatures from the tide pools—so popular that the marine life was being badly depleted. It is now protected, and although you may

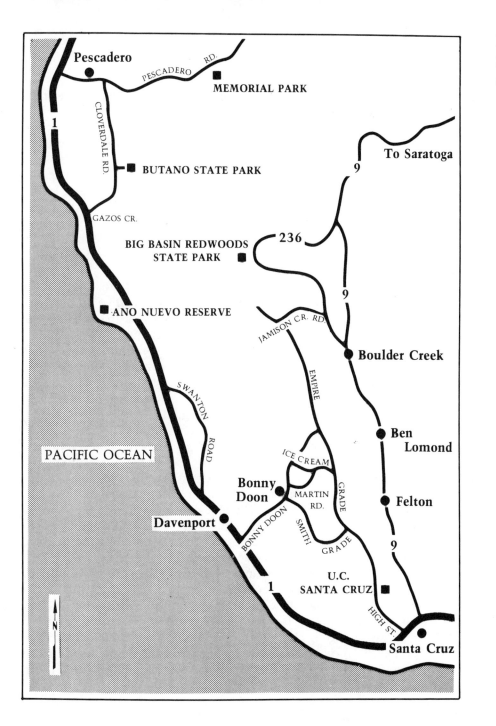

Pescadero,
Santa Cruz
and Empire Grade

131

not collect specimens it's a fascinating place for observation as you wander along the strange, rocky shore.

Two more miles south on route 1 is Princeton, to the right of the highway. Turn off and drive around the town. No matter how widely traveled you are, you'll never find another place that looks like this one. Most of the town seems involved in boat-building. The hulls of partly completed fishing boats are scattered about, high and dry, several blocks from the water. Everywhere you turn are boats of all vintages and types: old, new, decrepit, built of steel, wood, and concrete. There is a large marina, protected by a breakwater, facing south on Half Moon Bay. In earlier times Princeton was named Old Landing, a point for shipping local produce to San Francisco by schooner.

The Portolá expedition camped near the mouth of Pilarcitos Creek at the north end of Half Moon Bay on October 28, 1769. Here is the junction with State Route 92 (Half Moon Bay Road), which crosses the hills to San Mateo. It's heavily traveled, and we don't advise taking it. There are two other roads—slower driving but much less traffic—farther south, which we'll get to in due time. Half Moon Bay is an interesting town for a stroll, and the best place on this stretch of the coast for getting picnic supplies.

Just south of town is the first opportunity to get away from route 1 and travel along a county road. Turn left on the Higgins-Purisima Road, where Main Street meets the highway. In less than a mile you will see a boarded-up house sitting on a rise to the right of the road. It's the James Johnston house, a New England 'salt box' type, built in the 1850s by one of the earliest American settlers in this region. It's on private land, and you can only view it from afar. There's an informative historical sign on the right, across the road from a farmhouse. The road continues along a creek past a number of farmhouses, some recent but others dating from the last century. In a couple of miles you climb out of the valley on a winding road, two miles of which are unpaved but smooth.

There was once a town of Purisima, on the hill above the north bank of the creek just before your road reaches route 1 again. On the left, above the road, you can glimpse the old cemetery, and on the right is the recently burned former schoolhouse. If you actually get to route 1 you've gone too far. Turn around and go back half a mile to Verde Road, which you follow south for a mile. Avoid route 1 whenever you can. Where Verde Road comes to route 1, the Lobitas Creek Road goes left up the hill. Take it, and in about a quarter mile—*before* you cross a creek—a dirt road angles up to the left. Take that, which is still Lobitas Creek Road, even though it doesn't look promising. It quickly widens to a lane and a half, following along Lobitos Creek for a mile then crossing over and climbing into pastures and across rolling hills with grand distant views. It's one of the loveliest drives anywhere, and should not be missed—except in wet weather.

At the junction turn right to go back to the coast, either to route 1 or to continue south by back roads. (See the next tour: The Coast From Tunitas to Santa Cruz.) If you're making a loop to return to San Francisco, turn left. From this point it's about thirteen miles across the hills to the junction of Interstate 280 and State Route 84 at Woodside.

This is the least traveled of all the routes between the coast and the south end of San Francisco Bay. Tunitas Creek Road climbs up through a cool redwood forest. The road is narrow and has no center line, but the light traffic makes it not difficult. In about six miles you come to Skyline Boulevard (State Route 35) on top of the ridge. Go straight across and descend on Kings Mountain Road. This is steep and winding, but with a good surface and a center line. At three miles, on the left, is the entrance to Huddart County Park which has several large picnic areas, hiking and riding trails, and a playground.

One and a half miles past the park entrance is the old Woodside Store, on the right. This is the only building in Woodside to have survived from pioneer days. It was built in 1854, at the time Woodside was becoming a lumbering center. There were fifteen sawmills within a five-mile radius of the store, which had a clientele of more than 1,000 lumberjacks who received mail and bought food and strong drink there. As you will see, the store isn't very large, but nevertheless it managed to sell everything under the sun. Now it is operated as a museum by the county, and the array of items will give you some idea of its former stock in trade: farm equipment, carpenter's tools, kitchen implements, patent remedies, soaps and perfumes, and much more. Stop in and see for yourself.

Continue on Kings Mountain Road seven tenths of a mile to the stop sign at Woodside Road, State Route 84. Turn left, and in one and a half miles you come to Interstate 280. If you are doing this trip in reverse, take the Woodside Road exit from 280 and go west.

The Coast
from Tuṅitas to Santa Cruz

You get to Tunitas by coming down State Route 1 from San Francisco, or by coming across from Interstate 280 at Woodside on Kings Mountain Road and Tunitas Creek Road. (See previous trip.)

The name Tunitas is the diminutive of *tuna*, which is not the fish but rather the Spanish word for the fruit of the prickly pear. The town once had the honor of being the southern terminus of the Ocean Shore Railroad. Passengers bound for Santa Cruz rode in carriages or automobiles the rest of the way.

From the junction of route 1 and Tunitas Creek Road go south on route 1 for almost three miles, and turn left on Stage Road, which is at the top of a rise. Start looking for it after you've gone two and a half miles so you won't miss it. This was the route of the coastal road before the modern highway was built directly along the coast in 1940-41—and before that it was the stagecoach route. In just a mile you come to the hamlet of San Gregorio, at the junction with State Route 84, which is a main route—heavily traveled —across the hills to Woodside and Redwood City.

The Petersen and Alsford General Store is at the junction. It's a store of the old country mercantile sort, stocking the usual run of canned foods and picnic supplies, but also the kinds of goods that can only be found in a rural community: woodburning stoves, a large selection of cast-iron cookware, halters and horse blankets. There is also a bar along one side of the store.

About 1912 a man named J. Smeaton Chase made a horseback journey from Mexico to Oregon, and wrote about it in a book entitled *California Coast Trails*. As he entered San Mateo County from the south he suffered "twenty miles of dreadful dust, but compensated by a grateful scarcity of automobiles and other traffic." When he reached San Gregorio he detected one reason for light traffic: ". . . the collection of wagons that were drawn up awaiting their drivers, who were circulating industriously from saloon to saloon." Things haven't changed much, except that San Gregorio is a smaller place than then and no longer a popular resort spot—merely a place you pass as you head for the beach.

Go straight across route 84 and continue south on Stage Road. You avoid a good five miles of route 1 by taking this curving road up and down over low hills. You pass Pomponio Road turning off to the left. It goes about three miles up a valley and deadends, but if you're in an exploratory mood —why not?

Two miles before reaching Pescadero you pass Willowside Farm through a grand avenue of the largest eucalyptus trees we have ever seen. Pescadero ('fishing place') was founded in the 1850s by Spanish-speaking people. Apparently it was named for the large number of speckled trout that were once found in the creek. J. Smeaton Chase checked into a comfortable inn here, then had an experience that will sound quite familiar to those who have often stayed in motels. "A party of bibulous sportsmen arrived during the evening and pervaded the place with noise and profanity. When I learned that the noisiest, thirstiest, and most obscene of the group was a banker of San Francisco, I congratulated myself that no funds of mine were in his keeping, and hoped that warning visions might be vouchsafed to his clients in their dreams."

At Pescadero, going to the right will take you, in two miles, to the coastal highway and Pescadero Beach. Going left and following Pescadero Road is another way to cross the hills to Woodside. At seven miles is Memorial County Park, in the redwoods. There are many picnic areas, easy hiking trails, a nature center, and various activities. (Day use fee is $1.00. No dogs, cats, or other pets are allowed.)

Another four and a half miles past Memorial Park is the junction with Alpine Road. Turn left, and in just over a mile you come to State Route 84. Woodside is ten miles to the right, and San Gregorio and the coast are eight miles to the left.

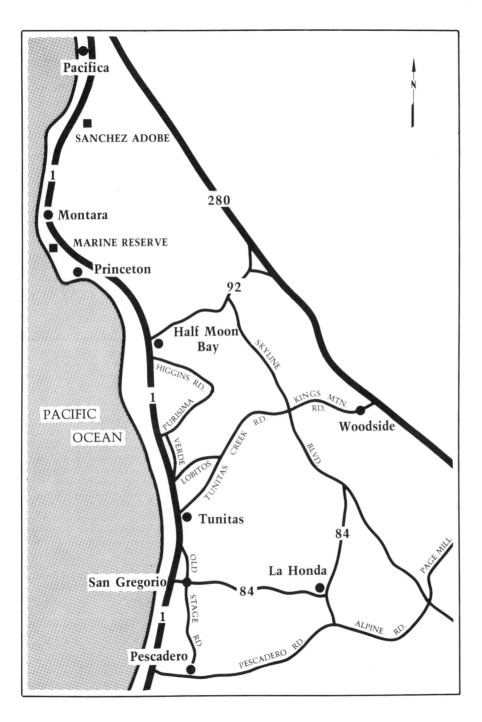

But to get back to the backroads tour. From Pescadero go left (east) for about a mile and turn right on Cloverdale Road. At the beginning this is a modern two-lane road running up a valley past artichoke fields and greenhouses for the production of commercial flowers. About five miles along is the turnoff to Butano State Park, which contains a small stand of virgin timber—the rest of these mountains have been selectively logged at one time or another. According to one source, *bútano* is what early Californians called a drinking cup made from a bull's horn.

After passing the entrance station the road goes into a dark, moist forest of redwood and Douglas fir, and in a mile ends at a campground that has picnic tables and restrooms. There are also some hiking trails. (Day use is $1.50, though if you are here on a winter weekday there may be no one around to take your money.) After you leave Butano and go on south you'll be on a gravel surface for about four miles to Gazos Creek Road. You turn right here to get to the coast highway.

Head south, and in five miles turn right on New Years Creek Road to Año Nuevo State Reserve. Año Nuevo is one of the few place names applied by an early navigator that has not been changed by later explorers or settlers. It was named by Sebastián Vizcaíno on January 3, 1603, since it was the first point of land sighted in the new year. The reserve is for the protection of elephant seals, sea lions, harbor seals, and several other species.

The male elephant seals arrive in December to battle for positions of dominance in the breeding season. The females begin to arrive around the first of the year, and give birth to their pups about six days after arrival. About twenty-four days after giving birth, the females are ready for mating. A few days after mating they wean their pups—by simply abandoning them and going back to the sea. The weaned pups, who have grown rapidly to weights of between three hundred and four hundred pounds, follow the adults back to sea by the end of April.

There is a one-mile hike you can make from the parking area to the point. It takes you along the beach, up a bluff, and past a field. It's spectacular scenery, and well worth taking a couple of hours for the round trip. If you're here during the elephant seal calving and breeding season (roughly December 1 to March 31) you will have to go on a scheduled guided tour. Reservations for the guided tours should be made by calling the reserve at (415) 879-0227 and 0228. The reserve is open from 8 A.M. to sunset, and a tour takes about two and a half hours.

A mile south of Año Nuevo you cross into Santa Cruz County, and two miles past the county line you turn left on Swanton Road. It's not marked, so keep your eyes open. The turnoff is just past the Big Creek Lumber Company. If you're coming from the south, turn right shortly after the Greyhound Rocks parking area. The name Swanton is certainly of more prosaic origin than the Spanish and Indian names that predominate on this coast. It's for Fred W. Swanton, who built a power house on a nearby creek.

Swanton Road was once the main highway before the present route 1 was built. It climbs steeply up a hillside, making several hairpin turns and providing great views up and down the coast. From the high point the road quickly descends into a forested valley, then comes into the open again and skirts dairy farms and fields of artichokes and Brussels sprouts. About five miles after leaving route 1 there is an old barn and some other buildings at the right of the road. Across from these, built into a hillside, is the "rock house," erected about 1870 by Ambrogio Gianone, an immigrant from Switzerland. It was used for making Swiss cheese. Gianone built well, as the walls of the structure look quite solid—though the wooden roof admits a good deal of daylight.

Back to route 1 again, and south one and a half miles to Davenport, a company town centered on a cement plant. Davenport Landing, just north of here, was established in the 1850s as a whaling station. Pull off the road across from the plant, and from the high bluffs you may be able to spot whales, which are close in at this point. The best time for whale-viewing is from late November through January.

A mile south of Davenport the Bonny Doon Road turns off to the left, and in three and a half miles climbs to meet the Empire Grade. Seven more miles down the coast is Santa Cruz. In October, 1769, the Portolá expedition came up this way, crossing half a dozen steep-sided ravines with great difficulty. It took them all day to cover a distance that the modern traveler does in ten minutes.

Zayante
and Mt. Charlie Roads

The major road from San Jose to Santa Cruz is State Route 17. For much of the way it is an undivided four-lane road following a curving route across the Santa Cruz Mountains. The traffic is particularly fierce on weekends and at the morning and afternoon rush hours during the week, and hardly seems to let up in midday. Some of route 17 is unavoidable, but from the Santa Clara–Santa Cruz county line south to Santa Cruz there are several alternatives both east and west of 17.

The ones west of 17 are reached by taking the exit at Summit Road, right at the county line. As you're headed south from San Jose, the exit ramp makes a sharp 180-degree hook to the right to a stop sign at Summit Road. Turn left, and in a very short distance turn left on Mt. Charlie Road—and you are now headed south again, parallel to route 17. But while the frenzied horde charges down route 17, you are off by yourself in a realm where another vehicle is a rarity and something to be remarked upon.

Charles Henry McKiernan, an Irishman who had been in the British Army and was plainly something of an adventurer arrived in California during the Gold Rush. After a stint in the mines he came to the Santa Cruz Mountains in 1850. He carved out a modest ranch near the summit, and achieved considerable skill as a bear hunter in defense of his stock. He was the only resident of the area for the first two years, and those who came later gave him the nickname Mountain Charlie. He built a number of roads and trails, and one of those became part of the stage route from Los

Gatos to Santa Cruz. This is Mt. Charlie Road, which is essentially unchanged since the early days except for the addition of pavement. It's narrow—one lane plus, but carrying two-way traffic—and with enough curves to make you keep your eyes on the road. Mountain Charlie's Ranch, which you pass soon after leaving Summit Road, is now a Christmas tree farm. Several miles down the grade you pass another old ranch which was once a changing station for the stage line. When you come to Glenwood Drive turn right, and at one mile go right again on Bean Creek Road. In about four miles this will bring you to Scotts Valley Road. Go right two tenths of a mile to a traffic light, Mt. Hermon Road. Left at the light takes you to route 17 and Santa Cruz. Right goes to Felton on State Route 9, about four miles.

Another fine drive from Summit Road to the Felton-Scotts Valley region is East Zayante Road. Exit from route 17 the same as for Mt. Charlie Road, turn left as before, and in about two miles turn left on East Zayante Road. A sign at the beginning says One Lane Road, which is quite true. Initially the road is a bit wider than that as it passes some houses, but then it narrows and descends steeply into the narrow valley of Zayante Creek. Although this road and Mt. Charlie Road are parallel and only about one and a half crow-fly miles apart, they are much different. Mt. Charlie Road is along a partly-wooded hillside with good views, and Zayante Road is in deep woods next to a stream which it crosses several times. Further, Mt. Charlie Road has an adequate pavement and can be driven in a downpour, but much of Zayante Road is unpaved or semipaved, and should be avoided in wet weather or immediately after a heavy rain.

About two miles before Felton, Zayante Road widens into a full two lanes with good pavement. There are many homes hidden in the trees, most of them in such darkness that you wonder if they ever see the sun. Follow Zayante Road to its end at Graham Hill Road. Go right about a quarter of a mile and turn left on Covered Bridge Road (there's a shopping center on the right). In a tenth of a mile is the Felton Covered Bridge, built in 1892 of local redwood. It's a state registered landmark, and you can't drive onto it—but you can walk. This is the tallest covered bridge in the country, although it's just 186 feet long.

Return to Graham Hill Road and head back the way you came. Go past Zayante Road, across the railroad tracks, and turn right for the Roaring

Camp & Big Trees Narrow-Gauge Railroad. The name says it all: an old steam-powered train, making an hour-long run over several miles of track through redwood groves and on steep grades to "Bear Mountain." The days the railroad operates and the frequency of its runs vary considerably with the time of year. (From early June through Labor Day it is open daily with the first run beginning at 11; open weekends and holidays year round, does State Route 9 from Felton. The names of roads and towns in this area illustrate the variety of sources for California place names: Santa Cruz is Spanish. Zayante apparently is Indian. Felton is named for Charles N. Felton, a late-nineteenth-century Assemblyman, Congressman, and U.S. Senator. Graham Hill Road is for Isaac Graham, a Kentucky frontiersman who came to California in 1833, bought land on Zayante Creek, and in 1842 built the first power sawmill in the state. Scotts Valley comes from Hiram Daniel Scott, who arrived at Monterey in 1846, and in 1852 bought a ranch in the valley now named for him. As for Mt. Hermon, you might wonder how the name of a peak in Palestine was transplanted to the Santa Cruz Mountains to clash with the names of early settlers and later politicians. Well, in 1905 a Christian group purchased a pleasure resort, and as pleasure was not their intent they appointed a committee to select a new name. The committee chose Mt. Hermon, which had the proper connotations; the old name simply wouldn't do. It was "The Tuxedo." (For the map to this trip, see p. 147.)

East of Route 17

The Summit Road turnoff from State Route 17 (see previous trip) also serves as access to several other alternative routes leading to Santa Cruz and Soquel. After making the 180-degree exit, cross over 17 and you'll be headed southeast on Summit Road. At just over three and a half miles turn right on Soquel–San Jose Road—often referred to as the "Old San Jose Road." This is a modern two-lane road, well known and given a fair amount of use. It was completed in 1858, and was a San Jose to Santa Cruz stage route. From the junction it's ten miles to Soquel, downhill all the way.

But don't rush down to Soquel just yet. There are other roads close by that aren't through routes from anywhere to anywhere else, which makes them desirable. From Summit Road come down the Old San Jose Road about six miles, and turn right on Laurel Glen Road—Casalegno's Market and Standard station are at the corner.

You now go back uphill for a bit over two miles and pass St. Clare's Retreat, operated by Franciscan Missionary Sisters. Just past the entrance turn left on Rodeo Gulch Road, which will take you to Soquel in five miles. At the start it runs along the top of a ridge having good views, then goes steeply down into a valley—or gulch—and runs through a semirural area to end at Soquel Drive. Soquel is seven tenths of a mile to the left from here, and downtown Santa Cruz is about three miles to the right.

A variation on that route is to continue past the turn to Rodeo Gulch

Road and go straight ahead on Mountain View Road to a three-way intersection, where you go left on Branciforte Road. The name comes from the Marqués de Branciforte, viceroy of New Spain in 1797 when a pueblo—now the city of Santa Cruz—was established across the river from Mission Santa Cruz. The pueblo was given the name of Branciforte, and the county too was called Branciforte for a brief time in 1850 before it was changed to Santa Cruz. Now only the road and the creek it follows bear the name Branciforte.

The road is good two-lane, running past rural homes and small farms. The speed limit is 35, there isn't much traffic, and what there is doesn't seem to be in a hurry. As you near Santa Cruz you will be next to De Laveaga Park for about a mile. There are several picnic areas along the creek, and an old covered bridge. The bridge, only 83 feet long, was built in 1892 and was in use until 1939. It was then moved half a block for the sake of preserving it, but it still spans the same creek and looks as though it had always been in that exact location. Branciforte Drive changes to Market Street which ends at Water Street in Santa Cruz. Turn right and cross the river to go downtown.

Another way to get onto this network of roads is to continue south on route 17 past the Summit Road turnoff. In five miles turn left on Vine Hill Road—from a left turn lane in the center. The turn is marked well in advance. Move over to the left lane and get your turn signal on so you won't be run over from behind. (There is also a big sign for St. Clare's Retreat.) Shortly after leaving route 17, Vine Hill Road jogs left at a fork, and in two miles comes to the three-way intersection with Branciforte Drive and Mountain View Road.

The most obscure route of all turns off Summit Road only about a mile after you've left route 17. Turn right at a crossroads sign onto Old Santa Cruz Road. There is no advance warning of the road name—just the crossroads sign. The road has an old concrete pavement, and you follow it just three tenths of a mile before turning left on Schulties Road, which is narrow, winding, and downhill. In a couple of miles you come to Laurel, once a busy lumber and railroad town but now reduced to a few houses. It lost its post office in 1953—the sure sign that a town has gone under. If you wonder how a town in this terrain could possibly have been on a railroad, just look around a bit. Laurel was on the South Pacific Coast Railroad

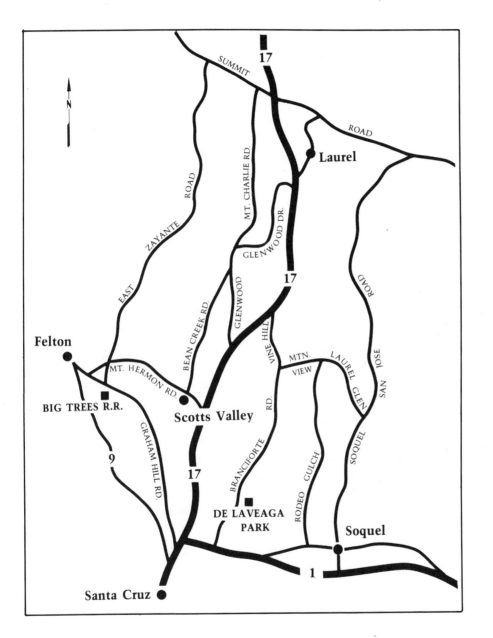

**Zayante and
East of Highway 17**

This old stage route runs through serene valleys and over low hills.

between Los Gatos and Santa Cruz, a narrow-gauge line completed in 1880. A mile-long tunnel began at Wrights, in Santa Clara County, and emerged at Laurel—to be followed almost at once by another tunnel which came out at Glenwood on the west side of route 17. The Southern Pacific Railroad took over the line in 1887, and converted it to standard gauge early in this century. The last train through Laurel was in 1940. From Laurel, continue on Laurel Road three miles to route 17.

On October 10, 1769, the Portolá party approached what is now called Soquel Creek, and saw "low hills well forested with high trees of a red color, not known to us." It was their first sight of redwoods, and they were amazed at the size. "Here are trees of girth so great that eight men placed side by side with extended arms are unable to embrace them." Those who came later also were amazed, and pleased at their good fortune. Soquel became a booming lumber town—until the redwoods were gone. Now the local crops are more prosaic: such things as grapes, fruit, and mushrooms.

There are three places in Soquel worth visiting to acquire those things that will please your eye and satisfy your taste buds. In order, from west to east, the first is a mushroom farm at 2875 Hillcrest Avenue. Hillcrest turns south off Soquel Drive a tenth of a mile east of where Rodeo Gulch Road comes in. (Turn at Norman's Family Chapel.) There is a retail outlet open 9 to 5, Tuesday through Saturday. Home gardeners can also buy compost Monday through Friday, 8 to 1; Saturday, 8 to 5. It sells for $2.50 a cubic yard, or $5.00 a pickup-load.

Back to Soquel Drive, turn right, and in six tenths of a mile you reach the traffic signal in the center of Soquel. On the right, several doors before the signal, is Maddock's Bakery, open Monday through Saturday, 5:30 A.M. to 5:55 P.M. They make excellent panettone, cookies (especially oatmeal crisps), and sweet rolls.

At the traffic signal go straight, and turn left on Main Street, the first street after you cross the creek. (This is just one long block past the signal, so be prepared.) Continue on Main to 3535, the Bargetto Winery—one of the few wineries remaining in this area. The winery was founded by two brothers in 1933, at the repeal of Prohibition, and is still owned by the family. There is a very attractive tasting room, open every day from 9:30 to 5:30. In back, overlooking Soquel Creek, you may spread out your feast of wine, bread, and mushrooms—and have at it.

Santa Cruz to Castroville

If you are overwrought, and feel the pressure of time, you can rush down the coast from Santa Cruz to Monterey in less than an hour on State Route 1. If you are calm and relaxed—or want to get that way—follow the directions below, and it may take you half a day to get to Monterey.

Leave Santa Cruz headed south on either the freeway—route 1—or on Soquel Avenue which becomes Soquel Drive as you cross the freeway. If on the freeway take the Soquel-Capitola exit, go into Soquel, and turn right on Soquel Drive. This was the highway before the freeway was built. It is by no means a country road, but merely a way to get you started on the proper route.

You will pass Cabrillo College, and soon arrive at Aptos. Go past the shopping center on the right, and at the three-way stop bear to the left under the railroad. Around the next bend is the older part of Aptos, a block of stores on the right, while on the left is the one thing worth seeing, the Bayview Hotel.

The Bayview was built in 1870, and was once a fashionable resort. (It was originally called the Ocean View Hotel, but no matter what the name, you can't see the water.) The hotel closed about 1915, and was deserted until the 1940s. It no longer rents rooms, but has a bar and dining room —and also some tables on an enclosed porch. (It's open Tuesday through Sunday. Lunch, 12 to 3, in the $2.50 to $3.50 range. Dinner from 5 to 10; $3.75 to $6.00.)

J. Smeaton Chase passed through Aptos, and stayed overnight—possibly at this hotel, as there may have been no other. To him, the name Aptos sounded Greek, but was nothing he could place. He asked the landlord who, or what, was Aptos. That gentleman replied: "Aptos, Aptos. Well, Aptos is a good name, ain't it?" Which once again proves that if you want to know something about a given locale, don't ask the natives.

Chase encountered some of the natives of his time, and was left with a feeling of disdain. "A quartette of Aptosians arrived after supper, to dangle for an hour about the porch and cultivate the social side by one of those friendly contests of mingled grossness and profanity which pass so often for wit in the rural life of the West." The next morning Chase rode "through quiet rural roads, and a village or two where loafers on sugar barrels were dallying with watermelons. . . ."

Even if you don't want to sample the Bayview's bill of fare, step inside to look at the fine old photographs on the walls in the dining area and the hallway next to the stairs. You'll notice that some of those pictured resemble Chase's "Aptosians"—and you'll agree that he had a point. Behind the Bayview is Village Fair Antiques, a complex of antique shops in one large building. (It's open Thursday through Sunday, 10 to 5.) The goods run from expensive furniture down to 78-rpm records and old picture postcards.

Continue along Soquel Drive to the next freeway interchange. Get on the freeway headed toward Monterey, and go to the second exit, San Andreas Road. Bear to the right at the end of the off ramp, and continue south on San Andreas Road toward La Selva Beach. There is some traffic at the outset, but within five miles most of it turns off toward one beach or another. When you get to Beach Road (a stop sign), turn left for a short distance then right at the next road—named Thurwachter Road here, but changing to McGowan Road in half a mile when you cross the Pajaro River, which is the Monterey County line. Pajaro, Spanish for 'bird,' was the name given in 1769 by members of the Portolá expedition who found a large bird that had been killed by Indians and stuffed with straw. William H. Brewer, who seems to have gone everywhere, came across the Pajaro Valley on August 2, 1861. He described it as ". . . a little bottom five or six miles wide and eight or ten long—a perfect level—an old lake filled in as is shown by its position and by the terraces around its sides."

Santa Cruz—Castroville

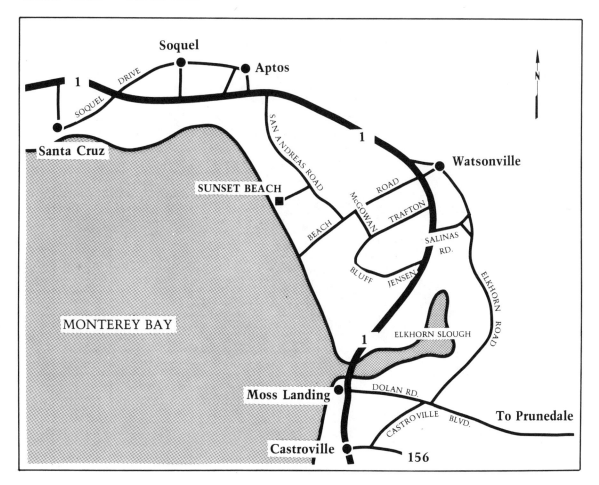

Soquel

Aptos

1

SOQUEL DRIVE

Santa Cruz

SAN ANDREAS ROAD

SUNSET BEACH

1

Watsonville

McGOWAN

ROAD

TRAFTON

BEACH

SALINAS RD.

BLUFF

JENSEN

ELKHORN ROAD

MONTEREY BAY

ELKHORN SLOUGH

1

Moss Landing

DOLAN RD.

To Prunedale

CASTROVILLE BLVD.

Castroville

156

N

In a field near Castroville,
"The Artichoke Capitol
of the World."

Turn right on Trafton Road at the end of McGowan, and follow around the end of a low hill through fields of Brussels sprouts and artichokes. In a mile or so you'll see the Bay View Mushroom Farm, a row of low white buildings on the right, with bales of hay and heaps of compost alongside. The farm sells mushrooms and compost on an informal basis. Just drive in and knock on the door of the office—morning hours are best.

Turn left on Bluff Road, and soon you'll come to Bluff Road Farms on the left, selling fresh eggs Monday through Saturday, 9 to 5. Left again at Jensen Road, and in about a mile you come to State Route 1. If you've had enough meandering around you can turn right, and charge off toward Monterey and Salinas—or Panama, if you keep at it long enough.

If meandering suits you, turn left and head back north toward Fairbanks, Alaska. At one mile turn right on Salinas Road, after another mile turn right again on Elkhorn Road, and after a short distance keep to the right at a fork. This is still Elkhorn Road; we just don't want you to succumb to indecision as you approach the fork. For several miles the road runs next to Elkhorn Slough, where there are always many water birds. After a couple of miles of slow going around curves you come to Castroville Boulevard. Turn right, and very shortly turn left and continue to State Route 156. Turn right, and in less than a mile you come to the junction with route 1. Straight ahead leads to Monterey. Right leads to Castroville, a place that bills itself as "The Artichoke Capitol of the World." That's probably not an exaggeration, as the area around Castroville grows 95 percent of the country's artichokes. Juan B. Castro founded the town in 1864. At one time Castroville had mainly a Portugese population, then mainly Swiss-Italian, and now it is mainly Mexican.

Highland Way-
Eureka Canyon-Corralitos

There is another road by which you can escape State Route 17, and eventually end up in the vicinity of Watsonville in southern Santa Cruz County. As you are headed south on 17 from San Jose, you will find a two-mile-long reservoir on your left soon after you have passed Los Gatos. At the southern end of the reservoir turn left on Old Santa Cruz Highway—the main road before the present four-lane 17 was built. Be alert. There is a lot of fast-moving traffic on 17. Get in the left lane well in advance of the turn.

Old Santa Cruz Highway winds uphill, and in about two miles you come to the Holy City post office on the left—in a long one-story building. You might stop here, and perhaps wander across the road to look at the several dilapidated and abandoned buildings—all that remains of Holy City, once the "headquarters for the world's perfect government." In 1918 William E. "Father" Riker, a perennial, unsuccessful candidate for governor, founded a religious colony here, based on a cult of white supremacy. At that time this was the main road from the Bay Area to Santa Cruz, and Holy City soon became a tourist attraction. In their heyday, Riker and his disciples operated a store, service station, restaurant, radio station, printing shop, and a mineral water business. The decline of Holy City began with the rerouting of the highway. The final blow came in 1966, when Riker, who was then ninety-three, brought an end to this utopian venture by joining the Roman Catholic Church.

A couple of miles past Holy City is the junction with Summit Road. Turn left, and in about a mile and a half turn right on Morrell Road. The last time we took this trip there wasn't a street sign to tell you where you were. Morrell Road is at the bottom of a dip just before a "School" sign. It winds downhill through dense woods, crosses the head of Laurel Creek, and winds back uphill to meet the Soquel-San Jose Road. At the stop sign go straight across, and you'll be on Miller Road headed toward Skyland, one mile away. This roundabout route is well worth your while, because at Skyland is a lovely Presbyterian Church, built in 1887. An unusual feature is a detached bell tower: a small, separate building containing the bell, with an exterior flight of stairs on one side.

Skyland might be said to have experienced genteel decline without having fallen into ruin. At one time it was a larger, more active community than it is now, with an economy based on lumbering, vineyards, and orchards. It hasn't had a post office since 1910, a good sign of how long it has been out of the economic mainstream.

At the church take the left fork, which goes uphill a bit then winds back down to Summit Road—which at this point has changed its name to Highland Way. Turn right, and for the next six miles you are traveling directly along the line of the San Andreas Fault. There are no dramatic signs of faulting—the heavy timber hides everything. This road carries light traffic on weekends, and almost nothing on weekdays. In the first couple of miles there are good southerly views toward Monterey Bay. Farther on you are in the woods, but the lack of a view is compensated for by many fine informal picnic spots, including several where streams cascade down over the rocks—at the right season. There is another name change—to Eureka Canyon Road—and the road follows Corralitos Creek down several miles to the crossroads of Corralitos (Little Corrals). In the 1860s the town is reported to have had a population of nearly 1,500, with the local economy based on cutting down the redwoods. Sawmills were moved from one location to another to keep up with the activity, and when the trees were gone the larger part of the population moved on.

At the crossroads—a stop sign—is the Corralitos Market and Sausage Company. They offer a dozen varieties of smoked and fresh sausage, ham, bacon, lamb, salmon, and turkey. No additives, fillers, or preservatives are used—one of the few places where you can escape the sodium nitrite and nitrate that seemingly are added to everything but wooden nutmegs.

South and east of here, at the appropriate season, you will find makeshift roadside stands selling local produce, and a number of places where you can pick your own fruits and vegetables at a cost of half or only a third of what you would pay at a market. Some of these places you will run across

Highland Way— New Almaden— Mt. Madonna

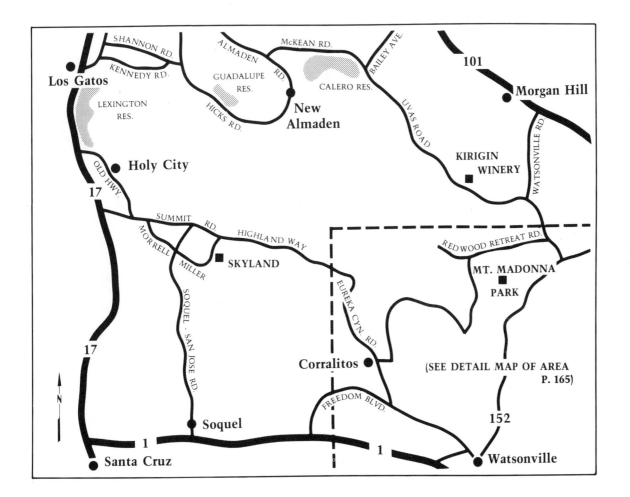

*This creek beside
Highland Way is a perfect
place to stop to have
a picnic lunch.*

simply by driving along the back roads. Others are established, and have signs out to attract would-be pickers.

As you came to the crossroads at Corralitos you were headed south. Turn left (east) on Browns Valley Road for three tenths of a mile to Amesti Road. Turn right, and in about three miles is Gurnee's Lakeside Farms at 600 Amesti Road. Turn left into Rianda Road, and follow the signs that have you check in to a garage. Strawberries, olallieberries, and boysenberries are the crops you can pick as their seasons come along; also raspberries in September. (Open 8 to 5, closed Mondays.)

Another good spot is Gizdich Berry Farms on Lakeview Road just off of Carlton Road. (Open 8 to 5.) There are strawberries in May and June, perhaps olallieberries later. Availability of such things as beans and tomatoes probably depends on how good a crop they have in any given year. There are several places on Peckham Road, off Carlton. Gizdich has apples here beginning in September. At 40 Peckham Road you can pick your own plums in July. If picking doesn't interest you, there is a good permanent produce stand on Holohan Road just west of State Route 152. It has great variety, and is clean and well run.

But of course if you make this trip at some other time of the year than harvest season, you'll need to know how to get from Corralitos to everywhere else. Turning right (west) at the crossroads takes you to State Route 1 north toward Santa Cruz. Straight ahead takes you, in one and a half miles, to a junction with Freedom Boulevard where you go left to Freedom and Watsonville. Left on Browns Valley Road for three tenths of a mile, and left again at the stop sign, has you at the end of the New Almaden–Mt. Madonna trip. If you have come from the vicinity of San Jose and want to make an all-day loop tour to return to San Jose, this is the way to do it. Locate the New Almaden-Mt. Madonna tour, turn the book upside down, and read the directions backward. If you get lost, go back the way you came.

New Almaden-Mt. Madonna

When you think of mining in California, gold and silver invariably come to mind. But the first great mining development in the state began in 1845, three years before the discovery of gold at Sutter's Mill. Quicksilver was the prize at New Almaden, and its discovery was a timely thing, as it is necessary for the reduction of gold ore. The mines at New Almaden are now closed, but there is a privately-run museum and tour to be had, and a quiet drive (part of it, anyway) that gets you there.

Head south from San Jose on State Route 17, take the second East Los Gatos exit, cross over 17 and go straight to the end of the road at Los Gatos Boulevard. Turn left, go about two tenths of a mile to Kennedy Road (the first traffic signal) and turn right. For about a mile Kennedy Road runs through a residential area, but then becomes a country road. After two more miles is a stop sign, Shannon Road, where you turn right and go another mile or so to Hicks Road and go right again.

Hicks Road winds up along Guadalupe Creek, and after the first mile the hills to your left are part of Almaden Quicksilver County Park—which has not yet been developed. You pass a reservoir, climb away from it and over a ridge, then down to the junction of Alamitos Road. Go left along the Almaden Reservoir, and in two miles you'll arrive at New Almaden. The word *almaden* is Spanish for 'mine' or 'mineral.' New Almaden was named for the famous Almaden quicksilver mine in Spain. The road bends to the left as you approach the town, but go straight ahead at the bend on

Bertram Drive. The New Almaden Food and Beverage Company—a restaurant and cocktail lounge—occupies an old house at the first corner. Just beyond is a community hall with a couple of weatherbeaten picnic tables next to it, and just beyond the hall is a historic monument beside the road. From the corner at the restaurant, cross the old narrow bridge to the main road. A short distance to the right is the New Almaden Museum. The owner, and conductor of most of the tours, is Constance Perham, whose family came here in the 1920s. (The hours the museum is open vary with the time of the year, but as a rule of thumb it is usually open weekends from 10 to 4; weekdays from 1 to 4; closed Wednesdays. If you want to make certain in advance that it will be open, phone (408) 268-7869. There is a charge, varying from 50¢ to $1.25, depending on one's age.)

Less than a mile on down the road is "Casa Grande," by far the most impressive building left from the old days. It was once the home of the mine superintendent, and was one of the great mansions of its time, with twenty rooms, wide balconies entirely around the lower story, hand-carved and inlaid fireplaces, and walls two feet thick. Today it contains a cocktail lounge done in the style of the 'Nineties, and a melodrama theater for weekend performances.

The much-traveled William H. Brewer, in his duties with the California Geological Survey, visited New Almaden in August, 1861. He said that the mine superintendent lived "in most magnificent style, like a prince." Brewer was given a guided tour of the mine by the mining engineer, and wrote:

> It is probably the richest quicksilver mine in the world, and is worth one or two million dollars. The pure red cinnabar (sulphuret of mercury) is taken out by the thousands of tons, and the less rich by the hundreds of thousands of tons. The mine is perfectly managed and conducted. The main drift is as large as a railroad tunnel, with a fine heavy railroad track running in. Six hundred feet in and three hundred feet below the surface of the hill is a large engine room, with a fine steam engine at work pumping water and raising ore from beneath. The workings extend 250 feet lower down. We went down. The extent of the mine is enormous—miles (not in a straight line) have been worked underground in the many short workings, and immense quantities of metal have been raised. We were underground nearly half a day, then came out and had a sumptuous dinner at a French restaurant. . . .

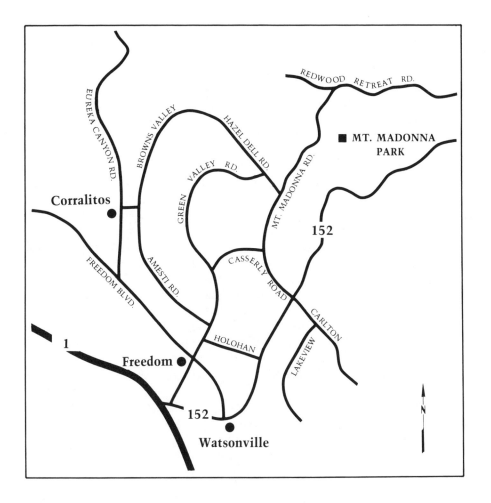

**Corralitos—
Watsonville Detail**

REDWOOD RETREAT RD.

EUREKA CANYON RD.

BROWNS VALLEY

HAZEL DELL RD.

■ MT. MADONNA
PARK

GREEN VALLEY RD.

MT. MADONNA RD.

Corralitos ●

152

FREEDOM BLVD.

AMESTI RD.

CASSERLY ROAD

CARLTON

1

HOLOHAN

LAKEVIEW

Freedom ●

152

N

Watsonville ●

Brewer reported the mine's output at about three thousand flasks (seventy-five pounds each) of quicksilver a month. More could have been produced, but that was all that the market could absorb. There were two other quicksilver mines nearby, the Enriquita and the Guadalupe, but neither was so rich and profitable as New Almaden. Brewer inspected them all, climbed Loma Prieta Peak one day, and was reluctant to leave, as there were several attractive young ladies in the vicinity, and also other forms of diversion. His final remarks on New Almaden were: "It was pay day yesterday, and last night the town rang with the sound of violins, guitars, dancing, *fandangos*, singing, and mirth."

About three miles after leaving New Almaden, turn right on McKean Road (county route G-8), the first major road you come to. There will be a fair amount of traffic on this one until you get past Calero Reservoir, a recreation area for powerboaters and water skiers. The name changes to Uvas Road (Spanish for 'grapes,' meaning a place where grapes grew wild.) Continue on Uvas Road, which is still G-8, ignoring roads to left or right. The way is through low rolling hills studded with oaks, and past another reservoir—this one unmolested by recreation.

At the junction with Watsonville Road turn right, and in a couple of miles on the left, at 11550 Watsonville Road, is Kirigin Cellars. This was formerly the Bonesio Winery. The buildings and grounds are exceptionally neat, and there is a very attractive tasting room open daily from 9 to 6. The oldest part of the family residence was built in 1827 of local redwoods.

From the winery it is less than a mile to where you turn sharp right on Redwood Retreat Road. (Straight ahead from this point for another mile brings you to State Route 152, the Hecker Pass Road.) Follow up Redwood Retreat Road for about three miles and turn left on Mt. Madonna Road. This is narrow and unpaved—but in fine shape—and winds uphill through dense woods to the intersection with Summit Avenue at the Santa Clara–Santa Cruz county line. Go straight across and down the other side, enjoying the great views of Monterey Bay—unless the bay is hidden by fog.

At the junction with Hazel Dell Road (a stop sign) at the foot of the grade, turn right. Hazel Dell Road, running past occasional old farms, goes right up the main fault valley of the San Andreas Fault. In about three miles you will come to the Hazel Dell school on the right. It's an old one-room structure, obviously abandoned some years ago. Though it's only a few feet from the road there *is* a fence in front of it, and it's on private property. You can admire and photograph it from the road, and there's room on the left to get your car off the pavement.

Roads have a tendency to change their names in this area, so don't be surprised when Hazel Dell becomes Browns Valley and then Amesti Road. Just keep straight on until it ends at Green Valley Road. Turn right, go through Freedom, and continue to the junction with State Route 152. Turn right here to go to State Route 1 headed north to Santa Cruz, and left to go to Watsonville. When Watsonville was laid out in 1852 the main local crop was potatoes. The first apple orchard was planted the next year, and Watsonville soon became the heart of the state's apple-growing region—as it still is. Roadside stands abound in September and October at picking time. Pippin, Gravenstein, and McIntosh are some of the favorites, as is the liquid form—cider by the gallon.

San Juan Bautista-
Fremont Peak-San Juan Grade

William H. Brewer visited Mission San Juan Bautista on a hot Sunday in July of 1861:

> I went to mass this morning in the Mission Church. It is a fine old church, with thick adobe walls, some two hundred feet long and forty feet wide, quite plain inside and whitewashed. The light is admitted through a few small windows in the thick walls near the ceiling, windows so small that they seem mere portholes on the outside, but entirely sufficient in this intensely light climate, where the desire is to exclude heat as much as to admit light—so the air was cool within, and the eyes relieved of the fierce glare that during the day reigns without.

The mission, founded in 1797, had been secularized in 1835, and by the time Brewer visited the town it had become an important stage stop on the San Francisco to Los Angeles route, being served by as many as eleven stage lines. The buildings that today face the plaza on three sides had already been built.

The mission still belongs to the Catholic Church, and can be toured even though it is not a part of the State Historic Park. The church is in use as the parish church for the town of San Juan Bautista, and though you won't see the same sort of congregation as Brewer saw, it is easy to imagine it as it once was.

The usual number of old and dingy paintings hung on the walls, the priest performed the usual ceremonies, while violins, wind instruments, and voices in the choir at times filled the venerable interior with soft music. . . . A congregation of perhaps 150 or 200 knelt, sat, or stood on its brick floor—a mixed and motley throng, but devout—Mexican, Indian, mixed breeds, Irish, French, German. There was a preponderance of Indians. Some of the Spanish *señoritas* with their gaily-colored shawls on their heads, were pretty, indeed. It is only in a Roman church that one sees such a picturesque mingling of races, so typical of Christian brotherhood.

Headed south from San Jose on U.S. 101 you reach San Juan Bautista by taking the State Route 129–Watsonville turnoff about ten miles south of Gilroy. Go left across the freeway and follow San Juan Highway four miles into town. As you enter town, turning on Second Street takes you to the plaza, while Third Street is the business street.

The various buildings facing the plaza comprise the state historic park, open 8 to 5 daily. For fifty cents you can walk through all the buildings: the Castro House, built in 1840-41, furnished in the style of the 1870s (when it belonged to the Breen family who were members of the Donner Party in 1846); the Zanetta House, built in 1868; the Plaza Stable, built about 1861, housing an interesting collection of old wagons, buggies, and other horse-drawn vehicles; and the Plaza Hotel, built in the early 1800s as a one-story adobe, and with a wooden second story added in 1858. The hotel is being restored to the way it appeared between 1858 and 1872, the years of its greatest prosperity. It is presently closed, and will reopen as a museum in 1980.

You can get an excellent informative pamphlet at the park offices in the Castro House. There are several delightful places to picnic—in the orchard behind the Castro House and the Plaza Hotel, in the gardens across the street from the side of the hotel, and behind the Zanetta House.

The mission sits atop an earthquake escarpment. From the open side of the plaza you look down a slope to a grandstand and rodeo grounds, and just there, at the foot of the grandstand, is the San Andreas Fault. The original El Camino Real—the Royal Road—that connected all of California's missions was also at the base of the slope. If you can afford to sit around long enough you may feel the fault move. If you're in a hurry, go down and stand on it briefly so you can tell your grandchildren of your courage.

At any shop on Third Street you can get a free copy of the visitors' historic walking tour guide. There are several antique stores, some cafes and tearooms, and a couple of markets, including the Paradis Bakery and

San Juan Bautista

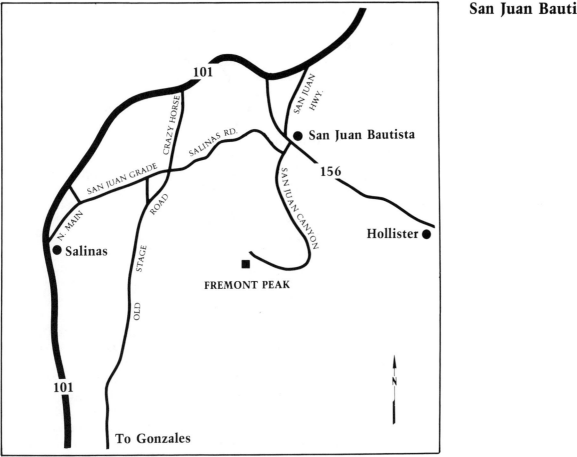

grocery store at the northern end of the business district.

Go south out of town on Third Street to the stop sign at route 156. Go straight across 156, taking care because the through traffic moves at a fast clip. Half a mile farther on is a fork in the road. Jog left and then right onto San Juan Canyon Road and head for Fremont Peak State Park.

Fremont Peak (more correctly Gavilan Peak, Spanish for 'sparrowhawk') is the highest point of the Gavilan Range on the boundary between San Benito and Monterey counties. Its popular name comes, of course, from John C. Frémont. In early March of 1846 Frémont and his small contingent of men were ordered to leave the country by the Mexican authorities. Instead, Frémont took his band to the top of Gavilan Peak, built a log fort, raised the U.S. flag, and defied the Mexicans to throw him out. Slowly, slowly the Mexicans, under the command of General José Castro, gathered at San Juan. Frémont held the peak for four days, then slowly retreated northward to Sutter's Fort. Obviously the battle that never took place was a victory for both sides. Frémont had defied the Mexicans for a short while without actually getting into a fight, and the Mexicans had got Frémont out of their territory. But like most inconclusive victories, the Gavilan episode created hard feelings on both sides, and is considered to be a direct cause of the Bear Flag Revolt that took place later in 1846.

Fremont State Park is open from 8 A.M. to sunset. (Day use is $1.50 per vehicle, camping is $2.00, and having a dog costs a dollar more.) From the beginning of the road near San Juan Bautista it is eleven miles to the parking area not far from the peak. It's a short, easy hike to the top—from ten to twenty minutes, and well worth it for the great view. And guess who's been here before you? You're right—William H. Brewer, who made the climb from town on July 2, 1861.

"We had a most magnificent and extensive view of the dry landscape—the Salinas plain, Monterey and the Santa Lucia, the sea, the hills north of Santa Cruz, San Juan and its valley, the valley of Santa Clara beyond, an immense stretch of landscape beside."

Return to the fork near route 156, and turn left on Salinas Road. In a short distance another road angles off to the left—Old Stage Road, the very route taken by stagecoaches between San Juan and Monterey as early as the 1850s. It is no longer passable across the hills, so continue on Salinas Road. For the next eight miles you will be driving on one of the few—or perhaps only—stretches of the original State Highway still in existence and in use. The first work on the concrete State Highway System was begun in San Mateo County in 1912. The road you are now on was completed across the low hills from San Juan to Salinas in 1915. At that time it was considered to be the last word in modern highway engineering. But the grade and the winding route soon became a bottleneck, and in 1929 the road was eliminated from the State Highway by construction of the "Prunedale Cut-off"—the route of present U.S. 101.

The old road is still used, though lightly, and receives enough maintenance to hold it together. You wind up toward the ridge crest at the Monterey County line—where the name becomes San Juan Grade Road —and another series of curves takes you down the other side. Some of the road has been repaved, but in places you will be driving on the original concrete surface—a remarkably durable road. This is especially true on the western end after you've come down from the ridge and the road has straightened out a bit.

Where the road widens into a modern two lanes is the intersection with Crazy Horse Road. Near here, on November 16, 1846, the Battle of Natividad took place. A group of Americans with a herd of several hundred horses were on their way to join Frémont at Monterey. They were attacked by a group of Californians led by Manuel Castro, and in the ensuing fight the Americans suffered four killed and four wounded. The Californians had somewhat greater losses. Though the battle decided nothing, it was the only engagement that occurred in northern California during the revolt of the Californians against the American military occupation.

If you want to go back north on U.S. 101, turn right on Crazy Horse Road and you'll come to 101 in less than four miles. If you are headed for Salinas or Monterey, continue straight ahead on San Juan Grade Road until it ends at North Main Street. Turn left here, which takes you to downtown Salinas, and—before downtown—an intersection with U.S. 101 freeway.

If you are going south on 101 and would like to avoid the freeway for a while longer, the Old Stage Road is what you're after. Turn left on Crazy Horse Road, and in less than a mile you'll come to Old Stage Road. This is the other end of the impassable road you saw near San Juan. Turn right, and drive past strawberry fields for a mile or so to a stop sign where you go left—but the name remains Old Stage Road. From here the road is mainly straight and modern to its junction with 101 just north of Gonzales.

To Help You On Your Way

You can enhance your pleasure if you are able to identify some of the flora and fauna. Instead of wondering idly what the name of that bird, flower, or tree is, you can look it up.

For the identification of birds, we recommend:
Peterson, Roger Tory. *A Field Guide to Western Birds.* Second edition. Boston, Houghton Mifflin, 1961.

For flowers:
Munz, Philip A. *California Spring Wildflowers.* Berkeley and Los Angeles, University of California Press, 1961.

For trees:
Watts, Tom. *Pacific Coast Tree Finder.* Berkeley, Nature Study Guild, 1974.

For berries:
Keator, Glenn. *Pacific Coast Berry Finder.* Berkeley, Nature Study Guild, 1978.

Other books of interest:

Chase, J. Smeaton. *California Coast Trails.* Boston and New York, Houghton Mifflin, 1913.

Dickinson, A Bray. *Narrow Gauge to the Redwoods.* Costa Mesa, California, Trans-Anglo Books, 1967.

Goss, Helen Rocca. *The Life and Death of a Quicksilver Mine.* Los Angeles, Historical Society of Southern California, 1958.

Hittell, Theodore H. *The Adventures of James Capen Adams.* New York, Charles Scribner's Sons, 1911.

Lyman, George D. *John Marsh, Pioneer.* New York, Charles Scribner's Sons, 1947.

Wagner, Jack R. *The Last Whistle.* Berkeley, Howell-North Books, 1974.

For information on the San Mateo County Park System, write or telephone:

Parks and Recreation Department
County Govt. Center
590 Hamilton St.
Redwood City, CA 94063
Phone: (415) 364-5600, Ext. 2486

For general information on the East Bay Regional Park District, write or phone:

11500 Skyline Boulevard
Oakland, CA 94619
Phone: (415) 531-9300

A free pamphlet entitled *California's Wine Wonderland*, a guide to California wineries open to the public, can be acquired by writing to:

Wine Institute
165 Post St.
San Francisco, CA 94108
Phone: (415) 986-0878

Other useful free guides to orchards and farms, some of which have U-pick fruit and vegetables:

Sonoma County Farm Trails
P.O. Box 6043
Santa Rosa, CA 95406

Harvest Time
(for eastern Contra Costa County)
P.O. Box O
Brentwood, CA 94513

Country Crossroads
(Santa Clara County)
Write to: San Jose Chamber
of Commerce
P.O. Box 6178
San Jose, CA 95150